THE POWER
OF NOTHING
TO LOSE

ALSO BY WILLIAM L. SILBER

The Story of Silver: How the White Metal Shaped America and the Modern World

Volcker: The Triumph of Persistence

When Washington Shut Down Wall Street: The Great Financial Crisis of 1914 and the Origins of America's Monetary Supremacy

Financial Options: From Theory to Practice (coauthor)

Principles of Money, Banking, and Financial Markets (coauthor)

Financial Innovation (editor)

Money (coauthor)

Portfolio Behavior of Financial Institutions

THE
POWER
OF
NOTHING
TO
LOSE

THE HAIL MARY EFFECT IN
POLITICS, WAR, AND BUSINESS

WILLIAM L. SILBER

WILLIAM MORROW
An Imprint of HarperCollins*Publishers*

HarperCollins books may be purchased for educational, business, or sales promotional use. For information, please email the Special Markets Department at SPsales@harpercollins.com.

FIRST EDITION

Designed by Kyle O'Brien

Library of Congress Cataloging-in-Publication Data has been applied for.

ISBN 978-0-06-301152-6

21 22 23 24 25   LSC   10 9 8 7 6 5 4 3 2 1

For Max, Ava, Dana, Shiloh,
and those in the pipeline

CONTENTS

THE POWER
OF NOTHING
TO LOSE

PROLOGUE
AN INVITATION

I have been thinking about this book for the past thirty years while teaching more than three hundred M.B.A. students each year at New York University's Stern School of Business. My course focuses on how investors choose among risky assets such as stocks, bonds, and real estate, but I soon realized that the same principles apply to presidents, generals, and ordinary people making decisions under uncertainty. A powerful result of the analysis: downside protection encourages normally cautious people to take daring chances. Let me explain.

The course is quite technical, so I designed a fun contest to sustain students' interest during the last few weeks of the semester, after the math has worn them down like a brutal running attack in a football game. I asked students to pick a stock or bond they think will earn the biggest profit during the last month of classes. They get 1½ points added to their final grade if they choose the winner, while losers receive nothing—except sympathy. How should they decide?

Some students agonize over the process, while the clever ones recognize quickly that this is like betting on who will win a home-run hitting contest: three-time All-Star Dave Kingman or Hall of Famer Willie Keeler. Kingman, who played during the 1970s and 1980s, batted a measly .236 and struck out about once every four times he came up to the plate. Keeler, his polar opposite, averaged a sizzling .341 over the course of nineteen seasons, from 1892 through 1910. He almost always made contact, striking out just once every seventy at-bats. But Dave dominated in home runs, slugging a four-bagger about once every fifteen trips to the plate, while Wee Willie needed 291 chances per homer. Keeler, who once summed up his hitting philosophy this way—"I hit 'em where they ain't"—was a much better batter than King Kong Kingman. But nobody cares about strikeouts in a Home Run Derby, just homers. Kingman should swing for the fences on every pitch, as long as strikeouts are not penalized, making him the best bet to win the contest.

Now back to the stock-picking game. No one knows the future, but the best strategy for choosing the most profitable stock discards caution and picks the riskiest security on the list— perhaps a Canadian gold mining company. The volatile mining company offers the biggest possible profit over the next month, the equivalent of a home run, and the largest potential loss. But all losses, no matter how bad, count the same. Points are not subtracted from the final grade for the worst return (although that is not a bad idea). The rules of the stock-picking game limit the downside, so students should choose the most volatile investment, which may not always win but gives the best odds of getting the 1½-point prize.

The stories in this book show how that same idea encourages bold undertakings more broadly and how that behavior has altered history. Each chapter is self-contained, like a short story, and includes chronicles of American presidents, generals at war, notorious dictators, and ordinary people.

The brief chapter in part 1 illustrates the power of limited downside with the Hail Mary pass in football and with a call option in the stock market. These widely diverse opportunities offer favorable skewed outcomes—high upside and little damage—to the quarterback and to an investor, encouraging each to go for broke like Dave Kingman. The five chapters in part 2, "Risky Confrontations," advance a step further, showing how asymmetric payoffs have emboldened normally reserved people when confronting three of the world's most persistent problems: racial discrimination, disease, and war. A seamstress, Rosa Parks, felt she had little to lose in protesting bus segregation in her hometown of Montgomery, Alabama, and corrected a long-standing injustice. World War I erupted in August 1914 and challenged U.S. president Woodrow Wilson, but his pursuit of a second term caused unnecessary wartime deaths. The chapter on asylum seekers in the twenty-first century tells how migrants hazard death to escape persecution and poverty, while host countries throughout the world deter them with roadblocks. The "Medical Crises and Pandemics" chapter shows that President Donald Trump was warned about a pandemic but failed to act.

In part 3, "Man-Made Disasters," the episodes deal with synthetic asymmetries similar to a Home Run Derby, where the rules can be changed. For example, if "home runs minus strikeouts" determines the winner, a different strategy emerges. Dave Kingman's propensity to swing and miss would hurt his performance, so the disciplined Willie Keeler might then be a better bet. The stories in part 3 are in the same mold but more consequential. Adolf Hitler in World War II and Nick Leeson, a rogue trader for London's Baring Bank, took catastrophic gambles that ended in disaster for all. Hitler and Leeson could have been stopped, however, if their adversaries had altered the incentives. Part 4, "Something to Lose," follows up with two examples of how to neutralize dangerous misbehavior with countervailing pressures. Prison authorities turn potentially violent inmates serving life without parole into model citizens by giving them something to lose, and the chapter on suicide bombers suggests a similar strategy might succeed in curbing terrorists' incentives to kill. The last chapter gets personal, showing how a nothing-to-lose attitude, if managed properly, can help make a successful career.

What started as picking winners in a stock market contest and a Home Run Derby has turned into a surprisingly powerful weapon for understanding behavior under uncertainty in life. Most of the stories show that downside protection in politics, war, and business favors the "deciders" but hurts innocent bystanders, creating tension between private and public interests. This book takes aim at the collateral damage.

PART I

INTRODUCTION

CHAPTER 1

DOWNSIDE PROTECTION

Forty-three-year-old Jennifer Sutcliffe screamed when she saw a thick diamondback rattlesnake coiled among the flowers in the backyard of her home near Lake Corpus Christi, Texas, on Sunday, May 27, 2018.[1] She and her husband, Jeremy, had been tidying up the yard before their daughter and granddaughter arrived for a Memorial Day cookout. Alerted by his wife's scream, Jeremy grabbed a shovel and decapitated the snake. Ten minutes later, he picked up the severed head to throw it away and felt the fangs sink into his hand. Finding himself in something like a Stephen King horror story, Jeremy struggled to remove the snake's head for almost a minute. Jennifer, a nurse, knew he needed antivenom. She helped her husband into the car and began the one-hour drive to the hospital. Along the way, Jeremy had difficulty breathing, began losing consciousness, and mumbled, "If I die, I love you."[2] Doctors explained later that he had gone into septic shock. All from a decapitated rattlesnake.

Christine Rutter, a veterinarian at Texas A&M University, understood why Jeremy needed four days in a medically induced coma and twenty-six doses of antivenom to survive. (The usual is two to four.) A severed snakehead can live at least an hour and delivers a more lethal bite than normal because the snake is in mortal danger. According to Rutter, its "adrenaline is maximized . . . so whenever they bite, they give it all they have."[3] She added, "It's almost like a Hail Mary pass in football."

A recent study of mating rituals in Asian spiders confirms the same behavior. The two genital appendages of the male orb web spider of the species *Nephilengys malabarensis* break off during sex and plug up the female to block others from copulating with her. The sterilized male partner guards the female after sex, which lasts about ten seconds, to ensure its paternity by preventing other males from loosening the plugs and slipping through. In a series of experimental trials in the laboratory, an international team of scientists showed that males without their reproductive organs, the so-called eunuch spiders, regularly defeated fully endowed rivals in staged battles that lasted about sixty minutes. The biologists concluded, "A eunuch guarding a female will respond . . . with maximal force when faced with an intruder. . . . A sterile male has no reproductive future and has nothing to lose."[4] The scientists filmed the experimental battles to confirm the aggressive behavior of eunuch spiders, so the curious can watch the uncensored videos for themselves—with the usual caution that some of the scenes may be too graphic for children.

Humans have little in common with spiders or rattlesnakes, but the survival instinct prevails among all species and often alters normal behavior. Aaron Rodgers, star quarterback of the Green Bay Packers football team, has won games with the Hail Mary pass, but that is not why he will make the Hall of Fame. He succeeds with disciplined decision-making, having learned early in his career not to throw interceptions. As he once explained: "I knew that from eighth grade, when I started playing football, and on, the only way I was going to be able to stay on the field was if I made good decisions and didn't turn the ball over."[5]

Rodgers has thrown four times as many touchdown passes as interceptions during his career, a much better ratio than superstar quarterbacks Tom Brady and Peyton Manning.[6] Nevertheless, Aaron Rodgers invites the chance of being picked off by throwing his signature pass into the end zone when Green Bay trails by a few points in the waning seconds of a game. Like the rattlesnake's severed head or the neutered spider, he has little to lose. The high upside with limited downside justifies rolling the dice because the desperate heave might notch a victory, but the otherwise certain defeat makes an interception meaningless. Rodgers's wager has an asymmetric, or skewed, payoff: substantial reward without significant negative consequence, turning the normally disciplined leader into a gambler.

Similar payoffs often arise in widely diverse activities, including politics, war, and business, with far more impact than Green Bay's Super Bowl prospects. History shows that the success of the American Revolution turned on such a venture. General George Washington prepared for combat like a chess grandmaster, designing tactics to anticipate his enemy's plans. On January 4, 1776, he asked the Continental Congress to reinforce New York: "I submit it with all due deference . . . whether it would not be consistent with prudence to have some of the Jersey Troops thrown into New York, to prevent . . . the landing of [enemy] Troops at that place or on Long Island near it."[7]

He followed up on March 13, 1776, with another appeal to prudence: "As New York is of such importance; prudence and policy require, that every precaution that can be devised, should be adopted to frustrate the designs which the Enemy may have of obtaining possession of it."[8] Yet on Christmas night, December 25, 1776, the general discarded caution and crossed the icy Delaware River in a daring attack on the enemy in Trenton, New Jersey.

Circumstance forced Washington's change of heart. The British, under the command of General Sir William Howe, had defeated the Continental army in battles on Long Island and in Harlem Heights and White Plains in the second half of 1776, and sickness and desertions had thinned Washington's ranks. A week before the battle, Washington wrote to his cousin in Mount Vernon, "Your imagination can scarce extend to a situation more distressing than mine."[9] He needed a victory to attract more recruits, adding: "If this fails, I think the game will be pretty well up."[10] On December 20 General Washington gave Congress a timetable for defeat: "Ten days more will put an end to the existence of our army."[11]

Washington embraced the dangerous attack on Wednesday, December 25, 1776, because he had little choice. He understood the challenge, writing to financier Robert Morris right before the Battle of Trenton: "Some lucky Chance may yet turn up in our favor."[12] Indeed, luck prevailed, and America benefited from the gamble. George Washington crossing the Delaware may not resemble Aaron Rodgers throwing into the end zone, but they are the same.

Limited downside emboldening normally cautious people may seem obvious, but attacking Trenton in the middle of the night was not Washington's only option. He could have withdrawn forces and waited until the spring to attack. It took guts to take the chance. Even Aaron Rodgers, with nothing at stake but a meaningless interception, needs courage with his desperate heave because three-hundred-pound defensive linemen try to pound him senseless before he lofts the pass.

Quarterback Joe Namath led the New York Jets to victory over the Baltimore Colts in Super Bowl III on Sunday, January 12, 1969. It remains the greatest upset in sports history, with the possible exception of the American men's hockey team victory over the Soviet Union in the 1980 Winter Olympics. Everyone loves an underdog, and some evidence shows that long shots reward their betting fans because they play the game with abandon.[13] Namath's Jets did precisely that because no one respected their chances. They entered the game as 18-point underdogs to the Baltimore Colts—an unprecedented spread from Las Vegas bookmakers, who ignored Namath's boast beforehand that the Jets would win the game outright, not just beat the spread. Few would remember his now-famous words, "I guarantee it," had not Broadway Joe played the game of his life.[14] Namath received the Most Valuable Player Award, a testament to his spunk in achieving victory against the odds and for providing long-suffering Jets' fans since then with their only Super Bowl victory. Asymmetric payoffs encourage daring behavior, but it takes skill, conviction, and courage to exploit the opportunity.

Time pressure causes the skewed outcome for Aaron Rodgers and George Washington, but limited downside alone, even without the endgame drama, promotes bold decisions. Joe Namath played the Super Bowl without restraint because everyone expected him to lose. In the financial world, where money, rather than life and limb, is at stake, a call option shines a spotlight on loss limitation. Myron Scholes, winner of the Nobel Prize in Economics for discovering, along with Fischer Black and Robert Merton, the formula for pricing options, said, "Insuring the downside [was] how I got interested in options."[15]

Most investors are cautious, dividing their wealth between cash in the bank and the stock market so they can sleep well at night. Too much in stocks causes insomnia. Nevertheless, investors embrace volatile securities when buying a call option giving the right, but not the obligation, to buy stock at a fixed price. Rights, without obligations, give call options a skewed payoff: profits increase with rising stock prices, but losses are limited to a fixed fee, called the option premium. This protection against big losses makes a sophisticated financier like Warren Buffett, or even a conservative investor such as the Dalai Lama, discard caution and favor a call option on a volatile stock with lots of surprises, up and down.

Sound strange? The same happens in Major League Baseball when a manager gives the green light to a batter facing a count of three balls and no strikes. The hitter then has the option—the right but not the obligation—to swing at the next pitch, which he tries to belt out of the park. Los Angeles Angels outfielder Mike Trout, a three-time winner of the Most Valuable Player Award during the second decade of the twenty-first century, and a leading slugger, said that when the count is 3-0, he often swings "wildly, trying too hard to hit the ball far."[16] The *Wall Street Journal* noted, "While it could result in outs . . . the added possibility of a double or a home run makes it worth the risk."[17] Investors and major leaguers embrace danger and swing for the fences when their downsides are protected.

S kewed payoffs encourage daring exploits, a chance to shine like the brightest star, and that can lead to misbehavior, with fallout requiring a collective response. Not for Aaron Rodgers or Joe Namath, who bear all the costs of their decisions, so they can do as they please without our concern—unless we root for the Packers or (unfortunately) for the Jets. But the calculation is more complicated for someone like George Washington. A defeat at Trenton would have dashed the dreams of all Americans, not just the military commander in chief, giving Washington's wager broader consequence.

A less honorable leader than General Washington might have gambled simply to capture the glory of victory, letting others bear the burden of defeat. For example, during World War II, Adolf Hitler startled his advisers by ordering a desperate counterattack, the Battle of the Bulge, in December 1944, to stem the Allied advance into Germany.[18] Vastly outnumbered by British and American forces, and with the Soviet Red Army closing in from the east, Hitler chose a reckless offensive, explaining, "The outcome of the battle would spell either life or death for the German nation."[19] The Third Reich would have been better off pursuing peace and avoiding the cost in lives and destruction of that roll of the dice, but no one could restrain Hitler.

Karl Marx and Frederick Engels concluded their 1848 *Manifesto of the Communist Party* with a call to arms: "Let the ruling classes tremble at a Communistic revolution. The proletarians have nothing to lose but their chains."[20] Those words inspired violent uprisings over the next century, but Marx and Engels failed to alert citizens to the subsequent tyranny. The ruthless agenda of the Soviet Union's first two leaders, Vladimir Lenin and Joseph Stalin, brought them power and fame, but the brutal experiment inflicted great suffering on the Russian people before it ultimately failed in 1991. The proletarians had much to lose even though they did not know it.

Donald Trump had never held public office, and the political establishment dismissed his chances of success in 2016. He had spent a lifetime in business following the motto "Protect the downside, and the upside will take care of itself," which he then applied to politics.[21] He gambled with an unconventional campaign of provocative slogans to "lock up" his opponent, Democrat Hillary Clinton, and to make Mexico pay for a border wall. He won with a populist attack on the entrenched elite and by promising prosperity. Other candidates throughout the world have gained power with similar strategies, including former cricket star Imran Khan in Pakistan, Jair Bolsonaro in Brazil, and Viktor Orban in Hungary.

The success of this populist approach in today's political environment comes in part from the public's perception of growing income inequality and a winner-take-all economy. The gambles offer hope for the masses who have little to lose in bucking the status quo, which is also why playing the lottery is so popular. But most people forget that those desperate wagers rarely succeed. The Hail Mary connects less than one in twenty times, which may be okay at the end of a football game, but not as a steady diet in life.[22]

No one knows what President Trump would have done had he been reelected in November 2020, but toward the end of that campaign, when his prospects looked dim, Alex Conant, a Republican strategist, said that the Trump world was at a dangerous pass: "The knives come out, the donors flee, and the candidate throws embarrassing Hail Marys."[23] And that was before Donald Trump incited a mob on January 6, 2021, to attack the Capitol Building in a desperate lunge to prevent Congress from certifying that Joseph R. Biden Jr. had won the election. He had underestimated the downside and paid for it. The U.S. House of Representatives impeached Donald Trump for "incitement of insurrection," making him the first president in American history to be impeached twice.

Everyone understands that a nothing-to-lose strategy promotes brazen behavior, courtesy of our sports-obsessed world, but this book widens the scope by showing how presidents, generals, and dictators have exploited that incentive, altering our lives. Decisions with limited downside in politics, war, and business often favor the few but hurt the masses, creating social discord. Mitigating that damage is easy to say and hard to do, like dieting and exercising, but insurance companies routinely confront a related problem called moral hazard, and their actions are instructive. State Farm and Liberty Mutual, for example, know that automobile insurance makes drivers less vigilant, either consciously or subconsciously, because the company bears most of the explicit cost of an accident, capping the insured's losses. Companies minimize the problem by altering incentives, including offering discounts for driver education certificates and by raising premiums for customers having too many close encounters with fire hydrants. Concerned politicians can do the same, changing the skewed payoffs to minimize the consequences of misbehavior, but the stories that follow show that this requires courage, and not everyone has been up to the challenge. We suffer the consequences.

PART II

RISKY CONFRONTATIONS

CHAPTER 2

LAME-DUCK
U.S. PRESIDENTS

R epublican presidents Richard Nixon and Ronald Reagan, and Democratic president Bill Clinton, all found trouble in their second terms. Nixon covered up the burglary of the Democratic National Committee headquarters in the Watergate Office Building in Washington, D.C.; Reagan admitted to trading arms for hostages in the Iran-contra scandal; and the U.S. House of Representatives impeached Clinton for perjury and obstruction of justice relating to his affair with White House intern Monica Lewinsky. Of the four U.S. chief executives elected to a second term during the last half of the twentieth century, only Dwight Eisenhower remained unscathed.[1]

Perhaps the explanation rests, in part, with the Twenty-Second Amendment to the U.S. Constitution that became law in 1951, barring U.S. presidents from serving more than two full terms, so they automatically become lame ducks after being reelected. They have less to lose in their second term without the ballot box to check their behavior. Lame-duck presidents want to preserve their long-term legacy, but the limited downside encourages them to accomplish that goal by taking more chances, including attempts to conceal earlier transgressions. Nixon, Reagan, and Clinton diminished their stature with those exploits.

Second-term presidents also misbehaved before the Twenty-Second Amendment because the two-term maximum had been an accepted tradition since George Washington. That unwritten rule was probably less influential in loosening restraints than the new law, but not for Democratic president Franklin Delano Roosevelt, a presumptive lame duck when reelected to a second term in 1936. During the previous three years, the Supreme Court had struck down key parts of his New Deal legislation intended to lift the country out of the Great Depression, and Roosevelt needed more sympathetic judges to move his program forward.

In early 1935, still in his first term, FDR considered ways to curb the court's power. Secretary of the Interior Harold Ickes described a cabinet meeting on Friday, January 11, 1935: "The attorney general went so far as to say that if the court went against the government, the number of justices should be increased at once so as to give a favorable majority. As a matter of fact, the president suggested this possibility to me during our interview on Thursday."[2] But pollsters considered the 1936 election too close to call, and Roosevelt played it safe, avoiding any mention of his plans for the court during the campaign.[3]

On Friday, February 5, 1937, three months after his landslide reelection, FDR proposed legislation to expand the Supreme Court to fifteen judges, saying it would "make the judicial branch of the government . . . function in accord with modern necessities."[4] Roosevelt's ambitious plan triggered a public outcry. The head of the American Bar Association, Frederick H. Stinchfield, said that to do so is "entirely out of line with what we have supposed to be the basic superiority and protection of our fundamental law, the Constitution."[5] Harry Bigelow, dean of the University of Chicago Law School said, "It is impossible to avoid the conclusion that the present plan is dictated, to a very considerable degree, by political considerations."[6] The editorial page of the conservative *New York Herald Tribune* alerted the country to an existential danger: "In this one hundred and sixty-first year of the independence of the United States, President Roosevelt has brought forward a proposal which, if enacted into law, would end the American State as it has existed throughout the long years of its life."[7] Financiers on Wall Street piled on by pushing down stocks more than 1.5 percent, almost double the normal daily movement in the market.[8] The press left no doubt about the reasons for the stock market sell-off, reporting that the chief executive of one big bank was "flabbergasted . . . at the drastic character of the changes proposed."[9]

A confident Roosevelt, flush with voter approval, expected support from his fellow Democrats who controlled the Senate and the House of Representatives. Congress had other ideas. The Senate Judiciary Committee rejected what became known as the court-packing bill, ending its report on the proposed legislation with a scathing denunciation: "It is a measure which should be so emphatically rejected that its parallel will never again be presented to the free representatives of the free people of America."[10] Roosevelt should have recognized trouble at the outset. His vice president, John Nance Garner, president of the Senate, held his nose and gave the thumbs-down when the bill was introduced in the Senate.[11]

Presidential historians attribute Roosevelt's controversial legislation to overconfidence, an affliction called the "sixth-year itch" when applied to other misbehaving commanders in chief during their second terms.[12] The voters had given Roosevelt an overwhelming mandate, and the lame-duck status freed him from restraint, both of which encouraged derring-do that resembles overconfidence. FDR should have known that his court-packing scheme was doomed when it failed Garner's smell test, but he plowed ahead as though he had little to lose.

E xamples of lame-duck presidents behaving recklessly hardly constitutes proof of a pattern. Some occupants of the White House misbehave from the start, while others would never ripple the rarefied air with a lifetime stay. Republican Warren Harding, elected in 1920, died during his first term and failed to see the avalanche of debris from his permissive politics. He appointed cronies to high office, such as Secretary of the Interior Albert Fall and Attorney General Harry Daugherty, and ignored their abuses of power. In contrast, Vice President Calvin Coolidge took over after Harding's death in 1923, was elected president in 1924, and stayed out of trouble by never saying much.[13] In one famous anecdote, perhaps apocryphal, a woman boasted to Coolidge that she bet a dinner companion she could get him to say more than two words. He responded, "You lose." Silent Cal breezed through his White House years and could have remained there forever without a whiff of scandal.

To show that downside protection emboldens lame ducks requires a clinical trial, as in a science laboratory, confronting a chief executive with similar dangers in both terms and comparing outcomes. Politics rarely provides such an opportunity, but history has been kind to us. A natural experiment confronted the twenty-eighth president of the United States, Woodrow Wilson, elected in 1912, reelected in 1916, and faced with World War I during both terms. His behavior carries a lesson for today's world powers.

homas Woodrow Wilson was born in Staunton, Virginia, in 1856, and grew up in Augusta, Georgia, where his father became a Presbyterian minister. He was called Tommy as a teenager; went to Princeton University, then known as the College of New Jersey; and graduated in 1879. He continued his studies at Johns Hopkins University in Baltimore, where he received a Ph.D. degree—making him the only president to date with a doctorate—and became an academic with the requisite pince-nez glasses. He married Ellen Axson from Savannah, returned to Princeton as a professor, and enjoyed the quiet life of an ivory-tower idealist, publishing scholarly studies, teaching, and avoiding manual labor. Wilson was drafted as president of the university in 1902 and, unlike most professors, became a successful administrator and fund-raiser. His growing reputation as an executive brought an invitation from the New Jersey Democratic Party to run for governor in 1910. Wilson won the election, breaking a five-term Republican Party hold on the governor's mansion, and the unlikely victory made him the Democratic presidential candidate in 1912. It was a swift rise to national prominence for an academic scribbler.

The 1912 election was unlike any American presidential contest before or since. The Republican Party convention in Chicago nominated William Howard Taft, the three-hundred-pound incumbent. Former president Teddy Roosevelt, also a Republican, who had served a partial term after William McKinley's assassination in 1901 and then won a full term in 1904, had battled Taft for the nomination at the convention. He ran under the banner of the newly established Progressive Party after he failed in Chicago. Of the three major candidates in 1912, only Democratic nominee Woodrow Wilson hadn't been president before.

Roosevelt and Taft split the Republican faithful, allowing Wilson to become president with only 42 percent of the vote. His lack of a popular mandate encouraged him to follow the country's isolationist sentiment when the Great War began in Europe in August 1914, pitting Britain, France, and Russia against Germany and Austria-Hungary. He delivered a message to the American people on Tuesday, August 18, 1914, saying, "Every man who really loves America will act and speak in the true spirit of neutrality, which is the spirit of impartiality and fairness and friendliness to all concerned."[14] The president sounded like a Quaker pastor but grounded his pacifism in the country's immigrant culture: "The people of the United States are drawn from many nations, and chiefly from the nations now at war. . . . Some will wish one nation, others another, to succeed in the momentous struggle. It will be easy to excite passion and difficult to allay it. . . . Such divisions among us would be fatal to our peace of mind." Wilson's neutrality balanced the interests of midwestern voters of German heritage against the Anglophiles of the Eastern Seaboard.

The president kept the United States neutral throughout his first term despite Germany's submarine warfare that killed Americans. The German U-boat that sank the British ocean liner RMS *Lusitania* on Friday, May 7, 1915, tested Wilson's commitment like none other. It was an unprovoked attack on an unarmed passenger ship, killing 128 Americans and violating the then-accepted rules of war guaranteeing safety to noncombatants.[15] Eyewitnesses inflamed public opinion by reporting lifeless bodies of women and children floating off the Irish coast, some missing limbs, their clothing torn to shreds. New York newspapers labeled it a "Crime Against Civilization," like the caption on a wanted poster.[16] But Wilson remained silent immediately after the attack, except for a statement released by his private secretary on Saturday night, May 8: "The president feels the distress and the gravity of the situation to the utmost and is considering very earnestly but very calmly, the right course of action to pursue."[17]

The provocation simmered.

H ollywood's spotlight on the 1912 sinking of the *Titanic* has overshadowed the *Lusitania* tragedy, but back then, the two calamities, separated by only three years, vied for the public's heart. Both ships were leviathans, almost three football fields long, could accommodate about two thousand passengers, had four giant funnels belching smoke, and could speed through the water at about twenty-five knots, although the *Lusitania,* known as the greyhound of the seas, was faster. The *Titanic* departed on its first, and last, journey from Southampton, England, and the *Lusitania* left from New York, but first-class accommodations on both ships resembled Park Avenue's Waldorf-Astoria. The passengers carried comparable pedigrees, including John Jacob Astor IV, who went down on the *Titanic,* and Alfred G. Vanderbilt, who drowned on the *Lusitania.* A fabricated story circulated that Vanderbilt had canceled his *Titanic* voyage a day before its departure only to sail on the *Lusitania.*[18]

Mystery surrounds the two great ships. According to a headline in the *Los Angeles Times:* "Owners Believed the *Lusitania* Could Not Be Sunk: Her Construction Was Better Than the *Titanic.*"[19] The failure of the *Lusitania*'s watertight compartments to keep the ship afloat confounded the experts. Two-thirds of the passengers died on each vessel, but unlike the *Titanic,* the *Lusitania* had enough lifeboats for all, so the fatalities should have been much lower. Deepening the puzzle: 72 percent of the women passengers perished on the *Lusitania,* compared with only 28 percent on the *Titanic,* apparently violating the maritime code of prioritizing the evacuation of women and children.[20] Eyewitnesses offered details.

Minutes before the submarine attack, at about two o'clock on a bright, sunny day in the Celtic Sea, with the green hills of the Irish countryside on the horizon, an officer on the bridge looked out on the nearly deserted deck of the *Lusitania.*[21] Lunch was being served in the dining rooms below, and the faint sound of music from an orchestra warmed the air. The ship advanced at less than top speed. Suddenly the officer noticed the wake of an iron pillar cutting through the water about seven hundred yards away. Recognizing the telltale sign of a submarine periscope as it slipped below the surface, he ordered a defensive maneuver—"Full speed ahead!"—to the engine room. But it was too late. He watched in horror as the bubbling trail of the onrushing torpedo headed toward the ship. Seconds later, an explosion rocked the vessel, shaking it like an earthquake and sending a giant geyser of seawater over the deck. The *Lusitania* listed to the starboard (right) side almost immediately, and an exploding boiler deep inside threw metal shards into the air, severing power lines and blackening interior passageways.[22]

Bruised passengers climbed the stairwells to the top deck, but many were trapped below. One survivor recalled muffled screams, like whimpering caged animals, from a fully loaded elevator stuck between decks.[23] There was no way to free them without electricity, but according to ship steward Percy Penny, those coming to the top seemed composed: "The shock was so sudden and so great that people scarcely had time to learn what happened. . . . There appeared to be an idea among the passengers that the *Lusitania* would not sink."[24] As the boat's list worsened, however, passengers headed for the lifeboats and found trouble.

Lifeboats on the *Lusitania*, like on many big ships, were suspended by ropes from a crane-like arm, called a davit, and were controlled by pulleys at each end of the small craft.[25] Crew members needed skill and coordination to launch successfully a packed lifeboat, like lowering a window washer's platform with fifty people down the side of a skyscraper. The list of the *Lusitania* made the task nearly impossible. Lifeboats on the starboard side hung too far away from the ship, dangling uselessly over the sea, while those on the port side angled into the vessel's interior and required heavy lifting to launch. The first boat that crew members muscled into place above the water set a bad precedent when a sailor lost control of the rope at the front end. The upended craft sent its occupants crashing into the sea sixty feet below.

Carl Elmer Foss of Montana, a slim and athletic physician on his way to Europe to work for the Red Cross, witnessed the crash.[26] Foss had jumped from the deck into the water wearing a life preserver, was a good swimmer, and was moving away from the ship when the lifeboat tumbled. He recalled: "Suddenly down came a boat from the davits with a crash. . . . It was smashed, and I noticed one man clinging for dear life from the wreckage. The propeller was revolving, and this poor fellow got his legs badly cut. . . . [He] hung tenaciously to a rope. The sinking ship still lurched forward, dragging the damaged boat with it." Many passengers witnessing the carnage from the deck decided to remain on the *Lusitania*, list and all, because they thought it safer than treacherous lifeboats.

Foss described the horror as the ship went down: "I saw two or three persons jump from the top of the stern. One of these was a woman. I heard no screaming, but as the great liner took her final plunge, there struck upon my ear a long, wailing, despairing, and beseeching cry."[27] There was nothing Foss could do but save himself. He swam a half mile to a canvas raft that was rescued later by a steamer, the *Indian Empire*.

Crew members launched successfully only six of the ship's twenty-two large wooden lifeboats before the *Lusitania* sank.[28] The ship disappeared eighteen minutes after the torpedo struck, a frantic heartbeat compared with the two hours and forty minutes the *Titanic* remained afloat after hitting the iceberg. The *Titanic* carried twenty lifeboats, too few to accommodate all its passengers, but the crew had enough time to implement the chivalric code of women and children first. Hollywood captured the honor of the *Titanic*, while history buried the tragedy of the *Lusitania*, and Woodrow Wilson shares the blame.

T he president had made no public statement after the attack, except for the May 8, 1915, press release, but was scheduled to deliver a major address celebrating naturalized citizens on Monday, May 10, to a capacity crowd of twelve thousand in Philadelphia's Convention Hall. The *New York Times* speculated "that the occasion will afford the opportunity for a display of feelings," but added, "nobody knows, of course, what will happen."[29] Few guessed that Wilson would completely omit mentioning the *Lusitania*, and fewer still anticipated his veiled reference to the ongoing war in Europe. Toward the end of his speech, delivered to an overflow audience, the president said, "There is such a thing as a man being too proud to fight. There is such a thing as a nation being so right that it does not need to convince others by force that it is right."[30]

A pugnacious Teddy Roosevelt, still smarting from his 1912 defeat and looking over Wilson's shoulder, ridiculed the president's words a day later, scoffing, "There are things worse than war," and wrote a magazine article whose headline characterized the attack on the *Lusitania* as "Murder on the High Seas." [31] Roosevelt compared Germany to "the pirates of the Barbary Coast . . . who were outcasts from among these civilized nations." He added, "But none of these old-time pirates committed murder on so vast a scale as in the case of the *Lusitania*."

Most Americans wanted the United States to remain neutral, but Wilson's closest adviser and confidante, Colonel Edward House, was an important exception. Independently wealthy, he was active in Democratic politics in Texas and received the honorific title of colonel from an appreciative governor. He joined Wilson's 1912 campaign as an adviser, and became a member of Wilson's inner circle and one of his best friends.[32] At the outbreak of the war, Wilson had sent House as a special emissary to European capitals. The colonel corresponded with the president almost daily, and on May 9, 1915, two days after the *Lusitania* sank, he sent the following telegram to Wilson from London: "America has come to the parting of the ways, when she must determine whether she stands for civilized or uncivilized warfare. We can no longer remain neutral spectators. . . . We are being weighed in the balance, and our position amongst nations is being assessed by mankind."[33] At a dinner party at the home of Walter Page, U.S. ambassador to Britain, House predicted, "We shall be at war with Germany within a month."[34]

The president had other ideas. His formal note to the German government on May 13, 1915, protested the loss of innocent life on the *Lusitania* and cited earlier violations of U.S. rights on the high seas, including German attacks on both the *Cushing* and the *Gulflight*, merchant vessels flying the American flag.[35] It demanded "a strict accountability" for attacks on U.S. ships and suggested that submarine commanders must have misunderstood their instructions because Germany could not have intended to destroy innocent lives. It demanded an end to all U-boat warfare against noncombatants.

Woodrow Wilson sounded like a kitten compared with Teddy Roosevelt's Bengal tiger, but he had a different perspective. Britain, too, had violated U.S. neutrality by confiscating alleged contraband from American merchant vessels bound for Germany, and the president wanted to appear evenhanded. He singled out Germany for a formal reprimand because American lives were lost, but the president knew that resentment toward Britain ran a close second to Germany, especially among U.S. citizens of German and Irish descent. Wilson, elected with only 42 percent of the vote, resembled a tightrope walker. He could not afford to antagonize anyone if he wanted to be reelected in 1916.

Germany pledged to end submarine attacks on unarmed passenger vessels but failed to deliver. Treasury Secretary William McAdoo, Wilson's son-in-law, recalled: "Following the sinking of the *Lusitania* and the ensuing controversy, the German government on September 1, 1915, assured the United States that 'Liners will not be sunk by submarines without [providing for] . . . safety of the lives of noncombatants'. . . . Yet within six weeks thereafter, the *Arabic* was sunk without warning, and three American passengers lost their lives." McAdoo continued the saga into 1916: "More protests and more lame explanations. . . . The sinking of harmless passenger ships went right on. . . . On April 18, 1916, we notified the German government that unless 'relentless and indiscriminate warfare against vessels of commerce . . . was brought to an end, the government of the United States can have no choice but to sever diplomatic relations with the German empire altogether.'"[36]

On April 25, 1916, Germany responded to the threat by promising to curb its submarines, saying, "We wish to avoid war," and that satisfied Wilson.[37] It was an election year, and the influential Colonel House, who had proposed war after the *Lusitania,* now changed his lyrics. He told the president he would lose against a unified Republican Party unless he captured the progressive voters west of the Mississippi River.[38] After the Republicans united behind Supreme Court Justice Charles Evans Hughes, House gave the president peace-loving tactics for the election: "It is the plain people that will determine the result, and we must get the issue properly before them. The keeping the country out of war and the great measures you have enacted into law should be our battle cry."[39]

The slogan "He kept us out of war" propelled Wilson to a narrow victory over Hughes on Tuesday, November 7, 1916. The *Chicago Daily Tribune* quoted a midwestern Republican state chairman as saying, "Enough Republican women voted for Wilson to throw the election. The reason for this was the specious plea 'He kept us out of war.'"[40] A *New York Times* headline declared, "Peace a Powerful Issue: 'He Kept Us Out of War' Won Women."[41] And the *Boston Daily Globe* wrote, "The women of California voted almost solidly for President Wilson. His policy of peace, Child Labor law, and other enactments that appeal to women won their support."[42] The Nineteenth Amendment to the US Constitution guaranteeing women suffrage passed in 1920, but twelve states permitted women to vote in the 1916 presidential election, and Wilson won all but two.[43] Women's preference for peace determined the outcome, but few realized that Woodrow Wilson himself knew it would not last.

A week after the election, on Tuesday, November 14, Colonel House arrived at the White House at six o'clock in the evening, and the president came to his room to talk, almost before the colonel had unpacked. House recalled that Wilson wanted "to write a note to all the belligerents demanding that the war cease" and asked for his opinion.[44] The president explained, "Unless we do this now, we must inevitably drift into war with Germany upon the submarine issue." Wilson believed "Germany has violated her promise . . . and that in order to maintain our position, we must break off diplomatic relations." A headline in the *Washington Post* the following week suggested the newspaper might have been eavesdropping on the conversation and proposed a political twist: "Election Clears Way to Act."[45] The news story elaborated: "While it is not evident that there will be any fundamental change in policy, freedom from fear that any move at all would be misinterpreted as motivated by internal political struggle has been removed." The implication was that Wilson now enjoyed the freedom of a lame duck to hazard war.

Three months after the election, on Saturday, February 3, 1917, the United States broke diplomatic relations after Germany announced it would begin unrestricted submarine warfare. Wilson recognized that Germany had repeatedly violated its previous pledges, but the press still called it the "greatest international crisis since the *Lusitania* was sunk."[46] Tension escalated a month later with the publication of a telegram from German foreign minister Arthur Zimmermann to the German ambassador to Mexico, Heinrich von Eckardt, outlining a bizarre plot to bring Mexico into the conflict.[47] The Zimmermann telegram proposed an alliance with Germany and promised financial aid to help Mexico "reconquer the lost territory in New Mexico, Texas, and Arizona." Wilson's secretary of state, Robert Lansing, dismissed its gravity, calling it "a stupid piece of business," but it was the final step in the two-year waltz to war.[48]

At 8:32 on Monday evening, April 2, 1917, President Wilson entered the House of Representatives to address a joint session of Congress. Members of the Supreme Court, the House of Representatives, the Senate, and the diplomatic corps, in formal evening dress, greeted Wilson with an ovation lasting more than two minutes.[49] When the applause ended, the president began by saying, "I have called this Congress into extraordinary session because there are serious, very serious, choices of policy to be made." Wilson described German violations of international law on the high seas since 1915 and then said, "Armed neutrality, it now appears, is impractical because submarines are in fact outlaws when used as the German submarines are used." After a pause, he added, "There is one choice we cannot make, we are incapable of making. We will not choose the path of submission."

At the word *submission,* Chief Justice Edward White, seated directly in front of the podium, put his hands above his head and clapped loudly. The press reported that the assemblage "followed him with a roar like a storm. It was a cheer so deep, so intense, and so much from the heart that it sounded like a shouted prayer."[50]

On April 6, 1917, a month after his inauguration, Woodrow Wilson signed the formal declaration of war against Germany. No one accused the president of acting hastily; if anything, many regretted the delay, suggesting that Wilson understood what should have been done much earlier. The *New York Times* editorialized: "The president now knows or is forced to admit what he must long have known, that Germany under the present dynasty, with its insatiable ambitions and its depravities of mind and heart, has never been our friend, can never be our friend."[51]

I n a retrospective on the war, future British prime minister Winston Churchill, recalling the brutal trench warfare that had buried ten million combatants, aimed a sharper arrow, blaming Wilson for unnecessary wartime deaths: "What he did in April 1917 could have been done in May 1915. And if done then, what abridgement of the slaughter; what sparing of the agony; what ruin, what catastrophes would have been prevented; in how many million homes would an empty chair be occupied today; how different would be the shattered world in which victors and vanquished alike are condemned to live!"[52]

Churchill, a great historian and politician, knew what had happened. Wilson dodged the war in May 1915 because he wanted to get reelected. The president's blatant strategy to remain in power lengthened the Great War and raised its staggering death toll.

Domestic politics in the United States had cost lives abroad, and not for the last time, but Wilson's behavior delivers another message. His willingness to act in 1917 shows the power of downside protection in freeing the White House from restraint. Americans elect a different commander in chief to a second term—a more bellicose one—even if he or she looks the same. Second-term presidents should come with a warning label: Do not provoke a lame duck.

CHAPTER 3

PARDON ME

Most state constitutions in the United States grant a governor the power of clemency: to show mercy by pardoning a criminal and wiping away the crime, or by commuting (shortening) a jail sentence. The practice traces back at least to the Middle Ages, when all homicides in England, even accidental deaths, were considered felonies, so the king could show mercy by pardoning those unjustly sentenced under rigid laws. In 1249, for example, four-year-old Katherine Passcavant was imprisoned because, in opening a door, she accidentally killed a younger child by pushing him into a pot of hot water. Katherine could not be acquitted by the courts and required the king's grace to avoid the gallows.[1]

Governors have done the same, but politics often interferes since commuting death sentences paints a candidate as soft on crime, a liability at the ballot box. The infamous Willie Horton commercial showcasing the furloughed Horton, a convicted murderer, committing rape and robbery, helped the sitting vice president, George H. W. Bush, defeat former Massachusetts governor Michael Dukakis in the 1988 presidential election. Dukakis did not free Horton but had simply supported the state's furlough program while in office, but it was enough to allow the

Bush campaign to tarnish his reputation. Bush crushed Dukakis 426 to 111 in the Electoral College.

The threat that a freed murderer will kill again restrains governors from granting clemency too easily, except when the state chief executives will no longer face voters.[2] Lame-duck governors are almost 50 percent more likely to commute the sentence of a death-row inmate compared with those who might stand for reelection.[3]

Risky behavior by second-term presidents, described in the last chapter, explains pardon leniency among lame ducks, but some governors and presidents have gone much further. Chief executives have abused their godlike clemency privileges by granting a flurry of "last-minute" pardons to well-connected but hardened criminals just days before leaving office. This recklessness suggests that some offenders are above the law, undermining the penal system, and serves as an example of collateral damage requiring countervailing action. Two instances of misbehaving governors confirm the problem.

On Monday, January 15, 1979, Ray Blanton, the outgoing Democratic governor of Tennessee, signed executive clemency documents freeing fifty-two prison inmates, including twelve convicted murderers. The most controversial was Roger Humphreys, a wealthy supporter's son convicted of murdering his former wife and her male friend by pumping eighteen shots into their bodies with a two-shot derringer.[4] A month earlier, the FBI had notified the forty-nine-year-old Blanton, elected governor in 1975 after serving three terms in Congress, that he was being investigated for selling pardons.[5] On Wednesday, January 17, in an emergency ceremony, the newly elected Lamar Alexander was sworn in as Tennessee governor three days ahead of schedule to avoid further last-minute pardons.[6] The new governor said that Blanton "disgraces the office," but could not reverse any of the actions.[7] Pardons are forever.[8]

Nelson Biddle, who worked for Blanton as a lobbyist, said of the governor: "He played hardball politics. You were loyal to your friends and hard on your enemies, and if you got the votes, then you called the shots."[9] When a reporter pressed Blanton on his record, the governor responded like a populist preacher: "Do you want a eunuch or some third-generation scion of a rich family who doesn't understand the problems of the poor?"[10] Biddle added to Blanton's antielitist credentials: "He grew up hating the establishment."[11] A Memphis newspaper called Democrat Blanton our "hillbilly Nixon."

Haley Barbour, the sixty-four-year-old former chairman of the Republican National Committee, showed in 2012 that GOP governors could also take advantage of last-minute pardons. Barbour had made front-page news when considering a presidential bid in 2011 but decided instead to complete his final year of two terms as governor of Mississippi. He made headlines of a different sort on Tuesday, January 10, 2012, his last day in office, by granting 193 pardons.[12] His immediate predecessor, one-term governor Ronnie Musgrove, granted just one full pardon, and the two-term governor before that, Kirk Fordice, a total of thirteen.

Local celebrities decorated Barbour's list. Burton Waldon, who belonged to a prominent, wealthy family known to contribute generously to Republican causes, had killed an eight-month-old boy in an alcohol-induced car crash.[13] Doug Hindman, son of a cardiologist from Jackson, arrested for exchanging hundreds of sexually explicit messages with an undercover officer posing as a schoolgirl, was the beneficiary of a plea for clemency by a personal friend of Barbour's. And Ernest Favre, convicted of killing his best friend in a drunken-driving accident, just happened to be the brother of Mississippi native Brett Favre, the Hall of Fame quarterback.

One editorial writer said that Barbour "very likely would have handed down fewer pardons if he were running for president now," a lesson learned courtesy of Willie Horton.[14] Barbour surely would not have pardoned David Gatlin, sentenced to life for shooting his estranged twenty-year-old wife in the head while she was holding her six-month old baby, and then wounding her friend Randy Walker. Upon hearing news of the pardon, Walker said, "I feel like my safety is in jeopardy. I wonder if he is going to finish what he started."[15] Gatlin said later, "I should never have gotten out of prison. God got me out."[16]

The Blanton and Barbour jailbreaks were the most egregious last-minute-pardon scandals in recent history, with the possible exception of President William Jefferson Clinton's performance at the end of his second term. Just a few hours before leaving office on Saturday, January 20, 2001, Bill Clinton granted 140 pardons and 36 commutations of sentence, prompting the *Washington Post* to write: "The extraordinary list [eclipsed] in magnitude and scope the last-minute legal forgiveness dispensed by previous presidents."[17] Roger Adams, a U.S. pardons attorney in Clinton's Justice Department, said, "I've never seen anything like this." Until then the president had granted four hundred pardons over eight years, or less than one a week. Clinton wanted to make up the shortfall and, on Thursday, January 18, 2001, had amused reporters during his last flight on Air Force One by jokingly asking the group, "You got anybody you want to pardon?"[18]

Bill Clinton ended his presidency like a cyclone, whirling around-the-clock during the last week, lamenting that he could not stand for reelection, but telling aides that if he remained continuously awake, "it would feel like four more years" in office.[19] He stuffed himself with his favorite comfort food (pizza and pastries); roamed the White House corridors, giving away autographs and memorabilia to the staff; and issued executive orders and regulations that filled nearly four thousand pages. But none of that frenetic activity compared with his last-minute pardons. Clinton labored all Friday night and continued well into Saturday morning, January 20, just hours before President Elect George W. Bush would be inaugurated, refining his recommendations. Red faced and bleary eyed, the president submitted a pardon list without any murderers (the commander in chief can forgive only federal criminal convictions), but with hubris that exceeded Blanton's and Barbour's.

For starters, Clinton pardoned his younger brother, Roger, who pleaded guilty to conspiring to distribute cocaine, and Henry Cisneros, his former secretary of the Department of Housing and Urban Development (HUD), convicted of lying to the FBI about how much money he gave a former mistress.[20] Ever the gentleman, Clinton also pardoned the mistress, political fund-raiser Linda Jones. And the president commuted the sentence of drug dealer Carlos Vignali, whose family had promised a $200,000 fee to Hugh Rodham, Hillary Clinton's brother, if the case was resolved favorably.[21] He also pardoned Susan McDougal, convicted of bank fraud in the Whitewater Development case, who was jailed for refusing to testify about Hillary and Bill Clinton's involvement in the failed real estate venture.[22] But Clinton's pardon of fugitive financier Marc Rich, and his lesser-known partner, Pinky Green, exceeded them all in damaging the judicial system.

Marc Rich, a sixty-six-year-old billionaire in 2001 who wore elegant dark suits, burgundy ties, and often smoked embargoed

Cuban cigars, had made a fortune trading oil with the enemy. Rich had been a successful commodities trader all his life, a swashbuckling adventurer who made a killing buying crude oil from Iran, contrary to American law since the 1979 hostage crisis, and reselling it on the world market. Charged by federal prosecutors in 1983 with racketeering, mail fraud, tax evasion, and violating the trading ban, Rich and partner Green faced three hundred years in prison if convicted on all counts. To avoid prosecution, the two men fled the country for Switzerland, the location of Marc Rich & Company corporate headquarters. Safe from extradition under Swiss law, Rich and Green had not returned to the United States since then. According to congressional testimony by Morris Weinberg Jr., former assistant U.S. attorney for the Southern District of New York and the lead prosecutor in the case, "The indictment was at the time the largest tax fraud prosecution in history," and the two men "were among the highest-priority white-collar fugitives in the world."[23]

Pressure for the pardons came from many Clinton cronies friendly with the runaways, but Denise Rich, former wife of Marc, and a million-dollar contributor to the Democratic Party, had the biggest impact. A talented songwriter with Grammy nominations to her credit, including hits for Celine Dion and Marc Anthony, Denise had befriended the president by donating $450,000 to his library fund, $100,000 to Hillary Clinton's U.S. Senate campaign, and $10,000 to his defense fund. When Bill appeared at a November 2000 benefit for a cancer research foundation in memory of Marc and Denise's daughter, she presented him with a gold-plated saxophone. He said, "Thank you for everything you've done to help Hillary and me serve."[24]

Denise Rich's letter to the president supporting the pardon said, among other things, "I am writing as a friend and admirer of yours to add my voice to the chorus of those who urge you to grant my former husband, Marc Rich, a pardon for the offenses unjustly alleged and so aggressively pursued."[25] Seated at the president's table at a subsequent White House dinner, she followed up: "I know you got my letter, and it means a great deal to me." Only Denise knows for sure why she helped her ex-husband, but she subsequently refused to testify in Congress about her role in the pardon, claiming Fifth Amendment rights.[26]

U.S. prosecutors were less reticent about appearing at the congressional hearings. Martin Auerbach, former assistant U.S. attorney in the Southern District of New York, who worked on the original investigation with Weinberg, testified afterward that there was no basis for granting the pardons: "I come here today to express the outrage I share . . . with many other Americans over President Clinton's pardon of Marc Rich and Pincus Green. . . . The notion that this pardon was, quote, on the merits, as has been said by our former president, a man who I voted for twice, is simply incorrect. . . . Mr. Rich and Mr. Green are commodities traders. By its nature, that is a gambling profession. And there is an old song about the gambler, which says, you have to know when to hold [and] know when to fold, when to walk away, know when to run. . . . And they ran because of the facts. And they couldn't come back because of the facts."[27] Auerbach then asked the congressional committee to make certain that future presidents never again "make the mistake" of pardoning fugitives who were in effect "thumbing their noses at American laws."

The press editorialized on the fallout of Bill Clinton's misbehavior.[28] The *New York Times* called his favor to Marc Rich, "An Indefensible Pardon," saying it was "a shocking abuse of presidential power" and "hardly what the Constitution's framers had in mind." The *Washington Post,* in a story headlined "Unpardonable," added, "With his scandalous present to Mr. Rich, Mr. Clinton has diminished the integrity and grandeur of the pardon power." The *Christian Science Monitor* summarized the damage: "The Constitution says the president can grant reprieves and pardons for offenses against the United States. Used rightly, this power can enhance justice. Used wrongly or questionably, it can undermine public confidence in evenhanded justice."

Congressman Barney Frank, a Massachusetts Democrat and a Clinton advocate during the 1998 impeachment proceedings, felt as though he had been slapped in the face by the Rich pardon: "It was a real betrayal by Bill Clinton of all who had been strongly supportive of him to do something this unjustified. It was contemptuous."[29] And as a member of the House Judiciary committee, Frank could do something about it. He fingered the timing of Clinton's decision, saying, "It strikes me that a large part of the problem is the pardons a president issues when they are beyond electoral sanction."[30] On February 27, 2001, less than two months after Clinton's housecleaning, Frank proposed a constitutional amendment that would prohibit a president from issuing pardons after October 1 in an election year through the following January 20, the day the newly elected president is inaugurated. The proposal would blunt last-minute pardons by giving voters the chance to punish the offending president's party. Frank thought the amendment had legs: "Ordinarily there isn't much chance . . . [but] I think, in this case, people might be sufficiently outraged."

A *Missouri Law Review* article, "Suspending the Pardon Power During the Twilight of a Presidential Term," added bipartisan flavor to Barney Frank's recipe by recalling Republican transgressions.[31] George H. W. Bush lost his bid for reelection on November 3, 1992, and then gave a neatly wrapped Christmas pardon to former defense secretary Caspar Weinberger on December 24, 1992, less than a month before handing the White House keys to Clinton. Weinberger had been scheduled to stand trial for lying to Congress in the Iran-contra affair. The next day, Lawrence Walsh, a former federal judge and the special prosecutor in the Iran-contra scandal, issued a statement suggesting the cover-up had serious consequences: "Weinberger's early and deliberate decision to conceal and withhold extensive contemporaneous notes of the Iran-contra matter radically altered the official investigations and possibly forestalled timely impeachment proceedings against President Reagan and other officials."[32] Walsh, a lifelong Republican, described the harm of the last-minute pardon: "President Bush's pardon of Caspar Weinberger and other Iran-contra defendants undermines the principle that no man is above the law. It demonstrates that powerful people with powerful allies can commit serious crimes in high office—deliberately abusing the public trust without consequence."

B arney Frank's twilight proposal to end lame-duck pardons faded into darkness. Some objections came from academics who argued that "a retiring president's liberation from political pressures may enable him to make politically unpopular pardons that are just and wise. The dispensation of such disinterested mercy is at the heart of the pardon power."[33] According to the professors, Frank's amendment would bar meritorious lame-duck acts of clemency along with the scandalous. They suggest that bad decisions make headlines, while the benign disappear into the archives of the Justice Department. Few remember that three days before leaving office, in January 2017, Barack Obama pardoned James Cartwright, a four-star Marine Corps general and former vice chairman of the Joint Chiefs of Staff, who pleaded guilty to denying falsely during a federal investigation that he leaked classified information to a *New York Times* reporter. Obama also pardoned Willie McCovey, the Hall of Fame San Francisco Giants first baseman who pleaded guilty to tax evasion for failing to report about $10,000 in income from sports card shows and memorabilia sales in 1995; McCovey died a year after being pardoned.[34]

Narrowing the lame-duck window might have prevented Bush and Clinton from abusing the system, but it would not have stopped the most controversial pardon in recent history. President Gerald Ford pardoned his fellow Republican, Richard Nixon, on September 8, 1974—four weeks after Nixon had resigned from the Oval Office in disgrace. Ford justified the pardon by saying it would end the "long national nightmare," but the press called it an "unwise, divisive, and unjust act."[35] Two days into the new administration, Ford's press secretary, Jerry terHorst, had assured reporters, "Mr. Ford flatly opposed any attempt to shield the former president from criminal prosecution."[36] He also reminded everyone that Ford had said during his vice presidential confirmation hearings in 1973, "I don't think the public would stand for it." When Ford pardoned Nixon, terHorst resigned in protest.[37]

Ford's flip-flop may have contributed to a changing of the guard at the White House, giving Democrat Jimmy Carter enough ammunition to edge him in the 1976 presidential election—a lamentable or favorable consequence, depending on party affiliation. But the pardon also created cover for future presidential misbehavior. Nixon got away with many sins, including his firing Watergate special prosecutor Archibald Cox—an outrageous move that was ruled illegal by a federal judge and set the stage for a constitutional crisis.[38] Nixon's escape from prosecution made it easier for Donald Trump to threaten firing special prosecutor Robert Mueller in 2018. He never did it, but the forty-fifth president tweeted a powerful broadside during Mueller's investigation into allegations of Russian meddling in the 2016 election: "As has been stated by numerous legal scholars, I have the absolute right to PARDON myself, but why would I do that when I have done nothing wrong?"[39]

Trump's tweet looks like fake news, but it is not as preposterous as it sounds. Legal scholars disagree over limits to the president's pardon power; some point to the absence of any explicit restraint in the Constitution, except during impeachment, to support Trump's claim, while others argue that a self-pardon puts the president above the law, which no one is. The Supreme Court ruled in July 2020 that New York prosecutors could subpoena President Trump's tax returns, overriding the president's claim that he was immune from such requests. Justice Brett Kavanaugh, a Trump appointee to the court, wrote in his opinion: "In our system of government, as this court has often stated, no one is above the law. That principle applies, of course, to a president."[40]

Nevertheless, Philip Kurland, the late University of Chicago legal scholar, who helped the Senate Judiciary Committee conclude that Nixon had obstructed justice, once summed up the literature on presidential self-pardon by saying: "Obviously, there's no answer."[41] Brian Kalt, a professor of law at Michigan State University said, "We can all only speculate what would happen if the president tried to do it . . . but no one can be sure."[42]

O nly a constitutional amendment could eliminate the pardon problem, and that is unlikely. But Congress could minimize the damage by borrowing an idea from state constitutions that modify a chief executive's clemency decisions with a review board. Establishing a public panel to bless or repudiate a president's pardons would restrain questionable decisions no matter when they occur, while permitting genuine acts of mercy through the end of a term. Only two states, North Dakota and South Dakota, give governors the same degree of unfettered discretion as the federal Constitution.[43] In thirteen states—Connecticut, Delaware, Georgia, Idaho, Louisiana, Minnesota, Montana, Nebraska, Oklahoma, Pennsylvania, South Carolina, Utah, and Washington—the governor appoints a pardon board that reviews clemency decisions and makes recommendations ranging from advisory to binding. In nine states—Delaware, Kansas, Louisiana, Montana, Nebraska, Oklahoma, Pennsylvania, Texas, and Washington—the governor can pardon only those proposed by the board.

A congressionally mandated pardon review board could not override the president's constitutional right to grant clemency, but it could resemble a speed bump on a busy street, slowing last-minute pardons that undermine the penal system while permitting safe passage to genuine acts of compassion. A public rebuke by an advisory board might have stopped Bill Clinton's proposed Marc Rich pardon, while allowing Barack Obama's sympathy for Willie McCovey to proceed. And Gerald Ford would have been less vulnerable to criticism with a pardon board to share the blame for having spared Nixon. A second-term president might still include his own name on a list of last-minute pardons, but that hubris is more than collateral damage. It could create a constitutional crisis.

CHAPTER 4

ASYLUM SEEKERS

On Tuesday, September 15, 2015, Doaa, a twenty-five-year-old Syrian, arrived at a makeshift refugee camp in Edirne, Turkey, near the border with Greece and Bulgaria, carrying her son Nassim. She had given birth to him a week earlier in Istanbul and had walked the last ten miles of a trek that began in Damascus, trying to escape the brutal civil war in Syria. Doaa refused to give her last name for fear of violent reprisals against her family back home but said with the persistence of a marathoner, "We're not going back. We're going to Europe even if we have to walk all the way to Germany."[1]

Doaa was not alone. She joined at least a thousand refugees determined to cross into Greece by land, a much safer trip than traveling by boat across the Aegean Sea to the Greek islands. They had seen the body of a three-year-old Syrian boy, Aylan Kurdi, lying facedown in the sand, washed ashore after his parents had tried to navigate the Aegean. Among those gambling with their lives to enter Europe via Greece were refugees with a different motivation. Thirty-year-old Amar Abdin also left Damascus for Germany, carrying a white tank top, shorts, and old basketball shoes. He said, "In every country, we dropped more of our stuff. I ended up with this T-shirt, and that's about it."[2] Amar worried about the safety of his group: "With every step you take, you risk your life. There are lots of people taking advantage of other people. We still can't believe we're doing this. We ask each other, 'Are we alive? Are we really doing this?'" Unlike Doaa, who feared persecution, Amar gave economic opportunity as his objective: "There's no life anymore in Syria. I had nothing to lose. But Germany is a great country. Business there is so good. When the crisis happened in 2008, the only country that kept growing was Germany."

The Turkish police tried to prevent refugees from crossing into Greece, rounding them up and returning them to Istanbul. The twenty-eight-state European Union offered more than $6 billion to Turkey in return for tightening its border restrictions— enough incentive to enlist the Turkish police as rent-a-cops to shutter the gateway to Europe.[3] Dursun Ali Sahin, governor of Turkey's Edirne Province, where the refugees gathered, said, "We took measures to guard the border and prevent people from crossing into Bulgaria and Greece. We're trying to convince people to go back to where they come from."[4] When a refugee complained, Sahin said, "If a country invites you, we'll help organize your trip there. So far, though, there isn't a single country which has officially invited you."

The European Union's payment to Turkey to bar Syrian migrants reflects a bias against foreign job seekers. A survey of eighteen thousand people in fifteen European countries shows anti-immigrant sentiment directed primarily against refugees wanting economic improvement, such as Amar Abdin, rather than those fleeing abuse, like Doaa.[5] But immigration officials wrestle to distinguish the two, and refugees with different objectives confound the problem with similar behavior, both often chancing death because they have little to lose. The confusion has created lethal harm, denying sanctuary to the persecuted because of the opportunists.

Some European Union member states have built fences to deter immigrants, including Austria, Bulgaria, Greece, Hungary, and Slovenia, but blueprints for physical barriers against foreigners have ancient roots.[6] Hadrian's Wall in England, an eighty-mile stone fence built during the second century, marked the northern boundary of the Roman Empire and separated the Romans from the barbarians.[7] Chinese emperors built the thirteen-thousand-mile Great Wall over two millennia for a similar purpose, to separate China from the barbarous people to the north. The lesser-known Offa's Dyke, an earthen barrier ordered by King Offa of Mercia during the eighth century, separated England from Wales and "bolstered Mercia's standing as a European power."[8] These structures had some military value but resemble more closely the scent markings of a wolf, warning potential interlopers to keep out. The difference is that humans use rocks rather than urine as a physical deterrent to foreigners.

Some countries enjoy natural barriers, reducing the need for artificial obstacles. The United States, for example, benefits from protection by the Atlantic and Pacific Oceans, and that encouraged its early tolerance of immigration. Foreigners with marketable skills could afford to make ocean crossings during the first half of the nineteenth century, so workers such as blacksmiths and carpenters, who could contribute to economic growth, dominated the immigrant flow.[9] The declining cost of ocean travel during the second half of the century lowered the effective barriers, encouraging a wave of unskilled immigrants from eastern Europe escaping economic deprivation and ethnic persecution. The resulting jump in the foreign-born population in the United States, from 10 percent in 1850 to more than 14 percent at the turn of the twentieth century, stoked an isolationist backlash in America.[10]

The U.S. Congress enacted the Immigration Act of 1924, raising a legislative wall to block undesirable immigrants from Europe and Asia. Republican Albert Johnson, representing Washington State's third congressional district, sponsored the bill that passed the House of Representatives by a vote of 323 to 71. During the floor debate, Johnson explained: "It has become necessary that the United States cease to become an asylum."[11] The legislation established strict quotas for potential immigrants of different nationalities, favoring those of British descent whose families had lived in the United States.[12] Republican congressman Fiorello La Guardia of New York said, "The mathematics of the bill disclose the discrimination against the Jews and the Italians."[13]

In the following decade, the anti-immigrant regime barred refugees fleeing persecution from Nazi Germany, including denying entry to a ship in 1939 with more than nine hundred men, women, and children that had to return to Europe as a result. That tragic incident, memorialized in the 1976 movie *Voyage of the Damned*, with an all-star cast of Faye Dunaway, Max von Sydow, James Mason, and Orson Welles, mobilized sympathy after World War II for displaced persons. An international conference in Geneva, Switzerland, in 1951 ratified a United Nations–sponsored agreement guaranteeing refuge for asylum seekers "persecuted for reasons of race, religion, nationality, membership of a particular social group, or political opinion."[14] The safe haven promised those fleeing oppression in the twenty-first century stems from this international agreement. Revisiting the doomed voyage of the steamship MS *St. Louis,* highlighting the desperate behavior of those threatened with death, might help modern immigration authorities identify those deserving sanctuary.

O n Saturday, May 13, 1939, the German ship *St. Louis,* owned by the Hamburg-Amerika line, and captained by fifty-four-year-old Gustav Schroeder, departed Hamburg for Cuba. On board were 937 passengers, almost all Jews fleeing Nazi persecution, who had purchased "landing certificates" from the director-general of the Cuban immigration office in Germany. Ten-year old Heinz Goldstein boarded the *St. Louis* with his parents, Hermann and Rita, and quickly found playmates among the nearly 200 children on the ship. He remembers a festive atmosphere, as though embarking on "a big adventure," enjoying the "chance to climb into the lifeboats, play hide-and-seek, and go into the captain's bridge with the other kids."[15]

Many of the adults, however, said tearful farewells to family members left behind. Aaron Pozner, a father of two, just released from the Dachau concentration camp on the condition that he leave the country, had saved enough for only one passage.[16] Before walking up the ship's gangway, he paused and cried while hugging his wife, promising to send for her and their children after he had made enough money. It would never happen. But many families boarding the ship felt relief, departing on a voyage to escape attacks that had escalated six months earlier after a violent upheaval called Kristallnacht, the "night of the broken glass," a reference to the smashed windows of Jewish-owned stores and synagogues throughout Germany. The organized destruction by Nazi thugs on November 9, 1938, and extending through the following day, left hundreds dead and marked a shift in Nazi persecution from economic strangulation to physical brutality, including public beatings, incarceration, and murder. The *St. Louis* resembled a magic carpet to freedom.

Nothing went according to plan. When the ship arrived in Havana Harbor on Saturday, May 27, 1939, the passengers celebrated as though it were New Year's Eve, but that was before Cuban president Federico Laredo Bru ordered the *St. Louis* quarantined, keeping its passengers on board. Laredo Bru denied the legitimacy of the "landing permits" sold by Cuban officials in Germany and, responding to earlier anti-immigration riots in Havana, decreed on June 1 that the ship depart for Germany the following day.[17] Friends and relatives of the passengers in Havana launched small boats, encircled the *St. Louis,* and shouted encouragement to the somber faces lining the railings above, but police attached huge searchlights to the sides of the ship to prevent anyone from rappelling into the friendly craft under cover of darkness. That did not prevent at least two passengers from trying to commit suicide, including Max Loewe, a lawyer from Hamburg, who slit his wrists and jumped overboard. A sailor rescued him, and Cuban officials sent Loewe to the General Calixto Garcia Hospital, but denied the request of his wife to join him to speak with the doctors. She remained on board, caring for their two children.

Heinz Goldstein recalled a cloud of despair smothering the ship: "I remember the anxiety that the adults experienced, the constant meetings, and constant update on what was being done to prevent a return to Nazi Germany. . . . Those were bad days. The mood was very somber. . . . Some of the people had already been in concentration camps, in deplorable situations."[18] One man, a former Vienna lawyer, showed his false teeth and explained that while imprisoned in Dachau "a member of the Gestapo [secret police] had knocked him down and stomped on his face, breaking every tooth."[19] Captain Schroeder worried about more attempted suicides and told the Cuban authorities that he would not be responsible for the safety of his remaining passengers. He counted 907 on board out of the 937 that left Hamburg: the Cuban government had granted entry as tourists to twenty-eight refugees holding American visas, Max Loewe was in the hospital, and one passenger had died on the voyage over.

The *St. Louis* left Havana at eleven thirty on Friday morning, June 2, destined for Hamburg, but Captain Schroeder, trying to avoid passenger suicides, diverted the ship toward the United States and anchored three miles off Miami.[20] A passenger committee sent a wireless message to the White House: "Cabling President Roosevelt, repeating urgent appeal for help for the passengers of the *St. Louis*. Help them, Mr. President, the 900 passengers, of which more than 400 are women and children."[21] The U.S. State Department responded that the refugees must "await their turns on the waiting list"—which was several years long.[22] The U.S. Coast Guard shadowed the vessel, recalled Harry Rosenbach, an eighteen-year-old passenger traveling alone on the *St. Louis*. His parents could afford only one passage, and the plan was for him to come to the United States and send for them later. "They wanted to save the children first," Harry explained, and then added: "I remember when we were off Miami Beach, and the Coast Guard ships were around us to make sure nobody jumped off. That was the message . . . until later, when I found out that the reason we didn't get in was because . . . it wasn't advisable politically. Nine hundred people in a country this big, and they couldn't find a place for us?"[23]

Denied entry into the United States, as well as Canada, the *St. Louis* sailed toward Europe, but Captain Schroeder stalled on the way back, refusing to return to Germany until he found a safe haven for his passengers. Acknowledged years later as a hero, Schroeder considered disabling the *St. Louis* off the English coast to force the British to rescue the refugees, but a last-minute agreement allowed the ship to dock in Antwerp, Belgium.[24] Four countries—Holland, France, Britain, and Belgium—divided the burden, each taking about 200 passengers, saving them from immediate German brutality. Captain Schroeder had no way of knowing that of those going to Holland, France, and Belgium, the Nazis would kill 255 in death camps after the Germans occupied those countries the very next year.[25] Even worse, the publicity surrounding the *St. Louis*'s futile voyage led to more deaths.

After Cuba rejected the refugees, another Hamburg-Amerika liner, *Orinoco,* carrying 200 Jews destined for Havana, received orders from Berlin to return home.[26] When the ship reversed course near Cherbourg, France, some passengers tried to jump overboard rather than face Nazi persecution. Others radioed a collective appeal to any country to admit them, emphasizing, "We have burned our bridges behind us."[27] The news headline "Refugees Returning to Reich as All Doors Close," summed up the international response. The *Orinoco* was the first of many ships that did not sail, leaving potential passengers to their fate in German concentration camps. Harry Rosenbach survived his odyssey on the *St. Louis,* but his parents, left behind, died in the Nazi death camp in Auschwitz, Poland.[28]

Asylum seekers in the twenty-first century who fear persecution at home can apply for refugee status in any of 148 countries that have signed the 1951 international conference guaranteeing the right of sanctuary. Unlike the refugees aboard the *St. Louis* who used suicide to make their case, they have the law on their side, but that does not make it easy. The list of countries offering a safe haven begins with Afghanistan and ends with Zimbabwe, but also includes one of the least populous in the world, Tuvalu, and the most populous, China, and almost everything in between.[29] The problem for most asylum seekers is to prove fear of persecution at home, as opposed to economic opportunism, and their prospective hosts are not always accommodating.

Ibrahim, a slim twenty-one-year old from the Darfur region of the Sudan, born into a wealthy family that lost everything in the ethnic fighting that plagued the area, crossed the Sahara and the Mediterranean—a three-thousand-mile obstacle course—on his way to Britain.[30] He arrived in the port city of Calais, France, in November 2014, separated from his dream by a twenty-mile trip across the Strait of Dover, but with almost no hope of clearing that final hurdle. Ibrahim was determined to better himself: "In Britain," he explained, "I can finish my education. Do I want to drive a rickshaw until I die? No, it can't be. If you want to change yourself, you must have an education."[31]

But that was the wrong answer for anyone seeking asylum. Signatories to the international agreement guaranteeing the right of sanctuary require proof of persecution. Ibrahim, who refused to give his last name for fear of hurting his chances, wanted to bolster his economic opportunities, but Britain, like other European countries, had more than enough domestic poor to feed. The roadblock forces refugees wanting better employment to try to sneak past the immigration authorities. Two months before Ibrahim arrived in Calais, a thirty-five-year-old Sudanese man crawled under a parked bus of visiting British schoolchildren and clung to the front axle for the return trip of 250 miles before collapsing in a Birmingham parking lot at the end. The press reported, "He was arrested on the spot."[32]

Britain is not alone in its skeptical treatment of immigrants. In October 1991 Abdalia Aziz Dukuly, a twenty-seven-year-old fleeing the civil war in Liberia, arrived in the Canary Islands, a Spanish archipelago in the Atlantic Ocean, seeking asylum.[33] He was told in Las Palmas, the capital of Gran Canaria island, that he must go to Madrid to present his case—an annoyance, but a small step considering the thousand-mile trip aboard a freighter that had brought him from Mauritania. He arrived in Madrid, went to the Spanish Red Cross office for assistance like other asylum seekers, and described his case: "My mother was killed in the fighting, and I made up my mind to come and hide in Europe. I lost my family, so I had nothing to lose."[34] Spain granted refugee status to only 7 percent of immigrants back then, but Dukuly fit the profile for acceptance. Felix Barrena, director of the Spanish Red Cross Center for Assistance to Foreigners, explained the difficulties for most others: "It's a social problem, not a racial problem, in my experience. People see refugees sleeping in the parks, and last summer some of them were caught selling drugs on the Plaza de España, and they make stereotypical judgments."[35]

Even compassionate Sweden, a nation of social workers, with a long record of open borders, has limited its indulgence. The Swedish Migration Agency decides which asylum seekers have "a well-founded fear of being persecuted," and assumes that just about anyone from Syria, Iraq, or Afghanistan, for example, deserves sanctuary. However, it usually denies applicants from Albania and Kosovo, suspecting that their motives are primarily economic.[36] Many Swedes are proud of their country's history of tolerance toward immigrants, although Paula Bieler, a member of parliament from the anti-immigrant Sweden Democrats party, told a reporter that the tolerant ones are "mostly the Swedes who haven't met them. It's the top politicians and journalists who live in the center of Stockholm."[37] A border policeman with daily immigrant contact said, "Last summer, my grandmother almost starved to death in the hospital, but the migrants get free food and medical care. I think a government's job is to take care of its own people first, and then, if there's anything left over, you help other people."

Australia's anti–boat people campaign to distinguish economic opportunists from persecuted asylum seekers makes Sweden's nationality test look good. Scott Morrison, who became Australian prime minister in 2018, had been the immigration minister in 2013 when the government announced Operation Sovereign Borders, a plan to use the military to divert boats with illegal asylum seekers before they reached Australian shores. Morrison vowed to take "every step necessary to ensure that people who arrive illegally by boat are not rewarded with permanent visas."[38] In an early incident testing the program, the Australian navy intercepted a boatload of 157 ethnic Tamils, refugees from Sri Lanka who had been living in India, and sent them to Nauru, one of the Pacific islands that Australia uses as a processing, or detention, center. Morrison explained, "The group were likely economic migrants who had been living in safety in India for some time."[39]

Australia insists that asylum seekers enter the country by air, with a valid visa, and then demonstrate that they are likely to be persecuted in their home country, a process that critics denounce. António Guterres, appointed secretary-general of the UN in 2015, and formerly the high commissioner for refugees, said, "Something strange happens in the minds of Australians when it comes to asylum seekers who arrive by boat without a visa.

Horrible instances of hundreds of people dying in unseaworthy boats may play a role in this thinking. So may xenophobia."[40] Salil Shetty, secretary-general of Amnesty International, is less forgiving, saying that Australia's maritime policy is "flagrantly violating" international human rights conventions, and cites the cost to the Rohingya people fleeing persecution in Myanmar as an example: "Do we know how many Rohingyas have died in the Andaman Sea because the Australian and other governments are refusing to receive them?"[41] Shetty describes the battle between asylum seekers and immigration officials similar to the futility of trench warfare: "No matter how high the walls or how well armed the coast guards, people who have nothing to lose will find a way to escape unbearable situations—even if it means risking their lives in dangerous journeys."

The Australian government under Prime Minister Morrison shows no signs of surrender. The commander for Operation Sovereign Borders appointed on December 14, 2018, Major General Craig Furini, outlined an uncompromising position: "I have a message for anyone considering illegal travel to Australia by boat: Don't. Australia's tough border protection policies mean no one who travels illegally by boat will ever be allowed to live or work in Australia." He then added details: "Australia recently intercepted thirteen people who unsuccessfully attempted to come here by boat. They wasted their money, needlessly put their lives at risk, and, as you can see, are now back in Sri Lanka and subject to further investigation by Sri Lankan authorities. I am committed to protecting Australia's borders, combatting people smuggling, and preventing vulnerable people from risking their lives at sea."[42]

On Friday evening, September 20, 2019, U.S. president Donald Trump hosted a state dinner, only the second of his presidency until then, to honor Morrison.[43] The guests enjoyed dining alfresco in the White House Rose Garden, decorated with huge yellow lights that warmed the humid air. The president toasted the Australian prime minister during the meal with a patriotic bear hug: "May our heroes forever inspire us, may our heritage always guide us, may our values always unite us, and may our nations always remain the home of the proud, and the brave and the free."[44] Morrison surely understood Trump's not-so subtle reference to united values. Three months earlier, the two men had met at the summit conference of world leaders in Osaka, Japan, and before the meeting, Trump said, "Much can be learned" from Australia's hard-line asylum policies.[45] The president had also given an appreciative wink to former Australian prime minister Malcolm Turnbull, saying, "You are worse than I am," in reference to his antiboat policy.

Scott Morrison's election sparked a calamity in the Australian-sponsored detention centers, giving him first place honors in the refugees' rogues gallery. Morrison spoke to his supporters at a victory party after the surprise win in the general election on Saturday, May 18, 2019: "I have always believed in miracles. Tonight is about every single Australian who depends on their government to put them first. And that is exactly what we are going to do."[46] Everyone understood his meaning, including asylum seekers in the detention center on Manus Island, Papua New Guinea, home to about six hundred migrants, mostly from the Middle East, caught trying to enter Australia by boat.[47] According to the press, "Within 48 hours of the election that returned Mr. Scott Morrison to power, the details of six suicide attempts start to emerge. Four of the men, including a Sudanese man who left a suicide note, ended up in the hospital. The two others were held by the police after they tried to set fire to themselves in their rooms."[48] Shamindan

Kanapathi, a twenty-eight-year-old Sri Lankan refugee on Manus, wrote in a text message to refugee advocates: "We are really devastated with the election results. We are really disappointed."

Suicide attempts on Manus Island in 2019, like on the *St. Louis* in 1939, send a message of despair, a desperate proof of feared persecution that should bring sanctuary to the asylum seekers. But doubts persist. According to Elaine Pearson, the Australian director for Human Rights Watch, who made several visits to Manus, "It's hard to know how many cases are serious cases of people trying to end their lives or a cry for help."[49] She then added, "In any case, it's a big escalation."

The cost of ignoring attempted suicides, even if staged, carries great danger, like the misstep in normally softhearted Sweden that ended in disaster. A research study of undocumented migrants in Stockholm reported that the Swedish Migration Board rejected without explanation the application of Fatemeh-Kian, "A 50-year-old Iranian transsexual . . . [who] fled from Iran because of her sexual orientation and had sought asylum in Sweden in November 2001. She had been arrested once by the morals police in Iran and had been sentenced to fifty lashes for homosexuality."[50] After a court hearing in Stockholm upholding the negative decision in February 2004, Fatemeh-Kian entered a detention center. The study followed up: "Abandoned and depressed, she attempted suicide in early May but was saved by other detainees. She was hospitalized overnight and was returned to the detention center the next day . . . accused of faking a suicide attempt. . . . On May 25, 2004, the staff at the center found Fatemeh-Kian dead in her room. Alone and disbelieved, she had committed suicide with antidepressants."

The 1951 Geneva agreement guaranteeing sanctuary for migrants remained silent on how to prove persecution, giving potential host countries a gap as wide as the Grand Canyon to manage or manipulate. All countries conduct interviews with potential immigrants but vary their criteria for granting refugee status according to supply and demand. For example, France responded to the increase in asylum seekers in the last quarter of the twentieth century by raising the bar for proper evidence. The French accepted 90 percent of asylum seekers when 2,000 applied in 1974, allowing an immigrant's word to confirm persecution. But when 61,422 knocked on the door in 1989, the country began to demand supporting medical certificates, and approvals plummeted to just 28 percent.[51] In 2001 a lawyer for an asylum seeker in France wrote to the client: "The CRR [Commission for Refugee Appeals] has informed me telephonically that it will make its decision only when it has been proved by a medical certificate that the marks on your body do in fact correspond to your account. For that purpose, you must *urgently* make an appointment with the doctor at the Avre, as well as a doctor of the Comede [Medical Committee for Exiles]. When you have the medical certificates of these two doctors, please fax them to me immediately."[52]

Civil wars and terrorism in the twenty-first century quintupled applications for asylum in the European Union between 2008 and 2015, increasing anti-refugee sentiment even in benevolent host countries.[53] Trying to distinguish applicants fearing persecution from those seeking better jobs gives immigration authorities insomnia. Restricting sanctuary to those with supporting medical records would work, but it ignores refugees with untreated psychological damage. Admitting only those who attempt suicide sets too high a bar and hazards being too late. It also overlooks evidence that opportunists are also ready to die.

Haitian men, women, and children pay smugglers up to $5,000 apiece—"a life's savings for most Haitians"—for a chance to work in the United States.[54] Smugglers often cram more than two hundred people into a boat on Grand Bahama Island, a way station for the trip to Key Biscayne, Florida. A news story from the South Florida Sun-Sentinal emphasized the danger: "The trips can be deadly. In May, at least 14 Haitian refugees drowned when their boat sank off the Bahamas. And in March 1999, 36 died as two boats sank 30 miles east of Palm Beach County."[55] John Philiph, a seventy-nine-year-old Haitian living in the Bahamas since 1963, said: "They can't find no work, they can't find no job, they can't make no money. . . . They don't have no help from no place, no country." Leatendore Percentie, secretary of the Grand Bahama Human Rights Association, explained the willingness of poor Haitians to chance death: "When you have nothing, you have nothing to lose."

Without a scalpel to separate the persecuted from the poor, countries close the door to immigration, and legitimate asylum seekers become collateral damage.

CHAPTER 5

ROSA PARKS

F orty-two-year-old Rosa Parks, a seamstress by trade but wearing a librarian's rimless glasses, became the standard-bearer of the civil rights movement in the United States by remaining seated on a Montgomery, Alabama, bus on Thursday, December 1, 1955, defying the driver's demand to cede her seat to a white passenger. Looking back sixty years later, her attorney, Fred Gray, said that the triumphant events following Parks's arrest "didn't happen by accident. It took meticulous planning and thought. It wasn't something that came together overnight."[1]

Later in life, Rosa Parks received accolades for her courage in the boycott that desegregated Montgomery's buses, including the Presidential Medal of Freedom and the Congressional Gold Medal. But a month after her arrest, she lost her job and eventually had to move to Detroit, where her brother lived, to find work. She reflected on her decision to fight Jim Crow: "I was not frightened. I just made up my mind that as long as we accepted that kind of treatment, it would continue, so I had nothing to lose."[2]

Parks, a proud woman with perfect posture, had lived in Montgomery and experienced racism her whole life, but she made the protest personal, switching from the collective "as long as *we* accepted that kind of treatment" to the singular, "*I* had nothing to lose." And that is because she carried a gene for promoting racial justice, an inheritance from her grandfather, Sylvester Edwards, and failure to act then would simply delay her mission. Her belief encouraged a perilous decision that delivered collateral benefits and altered history.

F red Gray, a bespectacled twenty-five-year-old lawyer, was too young to manage Rosa Parks's legal challenge to the Southern white establishment.[3] Born in Montgomery but denied the opportunity to attend all-white Alabama law schools, he graduated from Western Reserve University in Cleveland in 1954, and then opened a one-man office in his hometown.[4] With only two black lawyers in Montgomery, and more than forty thousand local African American citizens, Gray saw potential. He joined the local chapter of the National Association for the Advancement of Colored People (NAACP) and followed his heart, courting those seeking representation in civil rights cases. He knew that resentment among blacks toward segregated buses in Montgomery—where whites sat in the front seats and blacks sat in the back, and blacks paid the fare at the front door but entered at the rear—festered like an inflamed boil. African Americans commuted to work on city buses, unlike many whites, who could afford going by car, so blacks made up almost three-quarters of the ridership. Gray recalled making multiple bus trips a day during college: first, to and from classes at Montgomery's all-black Alabama State College, followed by a round-trip to his newspaper delivery job at the Advertiser Company, back to the library, and then home.[5] Daily complaints from black riders about mistreatment from bus drivers, who carried guns and enjoyed semipolice powers, chilled the air.

Georgia Gilmore, a midwife and a cook, told of the time she boarded the Court Street bus at South Jackson Street: "I tried to enter the front door, and the driver said, 'N——r, give me that money.' He then told me to get off and enter through the back door. While I walked to the back, he drove off without me."[6] Sadie Brooks, an official with the Women's Federation of Montgomery, recalled when a bus driver "whipped out a pistol and chased a colored man off the bus." And Mrs. Estelle Brooks said, "My husband was killed following a dispute with a driver." Those incidents may have been unusual, but Mrs. Veolo Bell resented the routine racism: "I have been on the buses many times to find colored people standing and ten empty seats in the front for whites." Mrs. Odessa Williams described a storm cloud smothering the black community: "They treated us like we were dogs."

Nine months before Rosa Parks, on Wednesday, March 2, 1955, an opportunity to challenge the indignities arose. Montgomery police arrested fifteen-year-old Claudette Colvin for the same offense that Parks would commit: failing to give up her bus seat to a white passenger. Colvin, who attended Booker T. Washington High School in Montgomery, explained what spurred her rebellion: "In my history class, when we studied the Constitution, I asked my teacher why we weren't given the same rights as others, since it was supposedly guaranteed to us too. . . . I never did get a good answer."[7] She then added, "As I grew older, I never could understand why we had to go to the back of the buses." Juvenile Court Judge Wiley Hill Jr. convicted Colvin, who wore glasses and weighed about ninety pounds after a full meal, of assaulting a police officer who removed her from the bus.[8]

Fred Gray, having waited for the right opportunity, met with her and thought this "could be the chance . . . to challenge the constitutionality of Montgomery's segregation ordinances."[9] He began to prepare the case, but Ed Nixon, known as Mr. Civil Rights in Montgomery, considered Colvin a weak plaintiff for the black community, and that mattered.[10]

Edgar Daniel Nixon, often called E.D., a Pullman car worker by trade, had been president of the local branch of the Brotherhood of Sleeping Car Porters, the union representing black railroad workers. Nixon's travels on the trains to other parts of the country exposed him to less restrictive racism compared with the Deep South and turned him into a civil rights activist at home. He had served as president of the local chapter of the NAACP, as well as of the state organization, and led the drive for black voter registration in Montgomery. Rosa Parks had become secretary of the Montgomery NAACP when Nixon was president, and he had helped her register to vote. She described him as a "proud, dignified man who carried himself straight as an arrow."[11] Nixon was fifty-five years old in 1955, and, according to Fred Gray, "If anybody ever had problems with the city police or any matter where they thought their civil rights had been denied, they would always contact E. D. Nixon."[12]

Nixon met with Claudette Colvin to see if she was the right person to confront the bus company. Although the teenager was prepared to fight, he thought she was too young, too emotional, and too feisty to represent the black community's case.[13] In retrospect, he says, "A whole lot of . . . people would think any . . . case, along with the person that was mistreated on the bus, would have made a good litigant. Well, my experience . . . taught me a whole lot different. I had to be sure that I had somebody that I could win with."[14] The legal battle would cost money, and Nixon felt Claudette would not inspire confidence, especially after he discovered that she was pregnant and unmarried.[15] The white press would have a field day with that information. "To be able to ask people to give us a half a million dollars to fight discrimination on the Montgomery bus line," he explained, "I ought to be able to say to them, 'We got a good litigant.'"

He found one on December 1, 1955, with Rosa Parks's arrest.

Rosa Parks, born on February 4, 1913, grew up in Pine Level, Alabama, a small community in Montgomery County, where her mother's family lived.[16] Her father, James McCauley, a skilled carpenter who travelled throughout the South building houses, was rarely home. Rosa recalls seeing him when she was about five years old but not again until she was an adult. Her mother, Leona, was a schoolteacher and spent weekdays with a family in the nearby village of Spring Hill, where she taught, leaving Rosa with her grandparents Rose and Sylvester Edwards. The two of them, born into slavery, made an impression on Rosa: her grandmother because she was so calm and unruffled, and her grandfather because he was so intense and passionate. She credited Sylvester, beaten as a child by an overseer on the plantation, with teaching her that "you don't put up with bad treatment from anybody," adding, "It was passed down almost in our genes."[17]

Rosa said her grandfather was light complexioned with straight hair, "and took every bit advantage of being white-looking."[18] She remembered his verbal combat: "He was always doing or saying something that would embarrass or agitate the white people. . . . He'd be introduced to some white man he did not know, and he'd say, 'Edwards is my name.'" Her grandfather compounded the subtle "offense" of using his last name by sometimes calling "white men by their first names . . . and not say 'Mister.'" Rosa knew that was dangerous because blacks were supposed to use their first names only and never to call a white person by name without saying "Mister" or "Miss." But Rosa learned that none of that talk matched the peril posed by her grandfather's belligerent backbone.

At age six, she watched Sylvester Edwards's stiffened stance in defending his home against the Ku Klux Klan. Racial violence erupted against African Americans returning from army service in World War I with dreams of breaking down the barriers of segregation, and Rosa understood that "whites didn't like blacks having that kind of attitude."[19] She said the Klan "was riding through the black community burning churches, beating up people, killing people." The violence got so bad, she recalled, "that my grandfather kept his gun—a double-barreled shotgun—close by at all times." She heard him say, "I don't know how long I would last if they came breaking in here, but I'm getting the first one who comes through the door." Grandfather Sylvester was not looking for trouble, according to Rosa, "But he was going to defend his home." The Klan violence subsided without further incident, and she sounded like a disappointed bystander when saying, "I wanted to see it. I wanted to see him shoot that gun."

Rosa Parks may have romanticized pulling the trigger at age six, but she showed restraint as a young adult. At nineteen, she met Raymond Parks, ten years older and a barber by trade, but shied away from seeing him when he came calling at her mother's Pine Level home. Like a typical teenager, however, she soon fell victim to his "little red Nash with a rumble seat in the back," recalling, "It was something special for a young black man to own his own car."[20] She married him in December 1932, moved to Montgomery, and says that Parks, as she called him, was the "first real activist I ever met."[21] Raymond Parks was a member of the Montgomery NAACP, considered a subversive group back then by southern whites, and Rosa believed, "He always did his best to get along, but whenever white people accosted him, he always wanted to let them know he could take care of business if he had to. They didn't bother you so much back then if you spoke right up."

Raymond discouraged Rosa from joining the NAACP in the early 1940s, thinking it too dangerous, but the absence of women in the Montgomery branch deterred her more. That obstacle disappeared when Rosa discovered that an old friend and former classmate at Mrs. White's Industrial School for Girls, Johnnie Carr, was a member. After Rosa joined, the two women renewed their friendship and founded the NAACP Youth Council in 1949 to attract young members.[22] That venture failed, but neither woman gave up, continuing to battle Jim Crow. Carr explained in familiar terms why blacks supported the rebellion, despite hardships, threats, and violent reprisals: "It was a rough time, [but] we had nothing to lose. Everything, everything in our community was segregated."[23]

Rosa Parks boarded the Cleveland Avenue bus at Court Square on Thursday evening, December 1, 1955, as usual after work, paid the ten-cent fare, and took a seat in the first row of the middle section—a no-man's land between the first ten seats reserved for whites, and the last ten for blacks. Under Montgomery's segregation rules, she had every right to sit there as long as the whites had enough seats, but if the front section filled up, the bus driver would ask the blacks to move. And that happened at the next stop, the Empire Theatre, when some whites got on and one was left standing.[24] The driver looked back at the row where Parks sat and said, "Let me have those front seats." When nobody moved, he added, "Y'all better make it light on yourselves and let me have those front seats." Three black passengers alongside Parks stood, but she remained seated, thinking about her grandfather's double-barreled shotgun, and watched the bus driver walk back toward her.[25]

Earlier in the year, Parks had discussed the case of Claudette Colvin, first with Ed Nixon and then during daily lunches with Fred Gray, whose law office was a couple of blocks from the Montgomery Fair Department Store, where she worked. After E.D. rejected Colvin, Rosa "knew they needed a plaintiff who was beyond reproach," but said, "I did not intend to get arrested."[26] Rosa did not start the day looking to protest bus segregation, but she admitted, "I was tired of giving in" after a lifetime of abuse.[27] Rosa recalled, "As far back as I can remember, I knew there was something wrong with our way of life when people could be mistreated because of the color of their skin."[28] Those thoughts swirled in her head, mixing with the sound of worried whispers among the passengers, as the driver walked slowly toward her seat. And then she recognized him: "a mean one . . . tall and thickset, with an intimidating posture."[29] Twelve years earlier, during the winter of 1943, that same driver, James Blake, had forced her to leave "my bus," as he called it, after she paid the fare but refused to enter through the rear door. This time, when he stopped beside her and asked if she was going to stand up, her grandfather's shotgun encouraged a firm "No." The driver then said, "Well, I'm going to have you arrested." Parks looked him in the eye and responded like a schoolteacher: "You may do that."[30]

Two policemen drove Rosa Parks to the jail on North Ripley

Street, where she was booked, fingerprinted, and photographed for mug shots—front and side views, like in the movies. She recalled: "I wasn't frightened . . . more resigned than anything else. . . . I was just prepared to accept whatever I had to face." After the formal charges, a matron escorted her to a cell, and, along the way, Rosa asked to use the pay phone in the hall. She called home, and her mother answered:[31]

"Hello."

"I'm in jail. See if Parks will come down here and get me out."

After a pause, her mother asked, "Did they beat you?"

Rosa remembered that the police had roughed up Claudette Colvin, so she said, "No, I wasn't beaten, but I am in jail."

Her mother handed the phone to Raymond. "Parks," Rosa asked, "will you come and get me out of jail?"

"I'll be there in a few minutes."

Many blacks knew of Rosa from her work in the NAACP and voter registration, so passengers from the bus spread the news while she waited in jail. Ed Nixon heard it from his wife, who heard from her neighbor, Bertha Butler, who had seen the police take Rosa from the bus. Nixon called Fred Gray to bail her out, but Gray had left town after lunch, so E.D. called Clifford Durr, a white attorney sympathetic to the cause. Durr's wife, Virginia, also a civil rights activist, knew Rosa from her work as a seamstress and was a sister-in-law of Supreme Court Justice Hugo Black, one of the longest-serving justices in U.S. history. Though Black had been a member of Alabama's Ku Klux Klan as a young man, he became an ardent supporter of civil rights on the court, including joining the unanimous 1954 decision in *Brown v. Board of Education of Topeka* to strike down racial segregation in schools. Virginia and Clifford Durr, along with Ed Nixon, went to the jail.

After they posted bail, Rosa walked through the iron mesh door from the cell area, flanked by two matrons, and saw Virginia waiting with tears in her eyes. Rosa thought she probably wondered what the police had done, and recalled, "She put her arms around me and hugged me as if we were sisters."[32] That familial embrace comforted her like a thick down overcoat. She still felt its warmth as she drove home with Raymond, saying, "I didn't realize how much being in jail upset me until I got out." Rosa told him they set the trial for four days later, Monday, December 5. They would need every minute of those four days to launch a rebellion that few expected to succeed, with the prominent exception of Montgomery's Mr. Civil Rights, E. D. Nixon, who turned Rosa Parks into a modern Joan of Arc and put Dr. Martin Luther King Jr. in the spotlight.[33]

E. D. knew what he had when they arrested Rosa Parks, having worked with her for many years: "Mrs. Parks was formerly my secretary in the NAACP, in the local branch for about twelve years," he reflected. "She also worked with me when I was state president of the NAACP. . . . If there ever was a woman who was dedicated to the cause, Rosa Parks was that woman. She had a deep conviction about what she thought was right. . . . I knew that she was clean as a pin. No one—nobody—could touch her morally. . . . The only thing you could say [was] . . . Rosa Parks just wouldn't get up and give that white man her seat. And that's what made me know that we could won [sic]."[34] He told Rosa she was the perfect plaintiff to challenge the constitutionality of bus segregation in Montgomery and then said to himself, "My God, look what segregation has put into my hands."[35]

Not everyone was so optimistic.

Rosa recalled that Raymond "thought it would be as difficult to get people to support me as a test case as it had been to develop a test case out of Claudette Colvin's experience."[36] Nixon had rejected Colvin as a weak plaintiff, but fear in the black community of economic reprisals by whites could have sidelined any protest. Raymond also worried about her personal safety, saying repeatedly to her, "Rosa, the white folks will kill you."[37]

He had good reason for concern. On Sunday, August 28, 1955, a little more than three months before Rosa's arrest, two white men mutilated and killed Emmett Till, a black fourteen-year-old from Chicago, visiting relatives in Mississippi. Till's brutal murder, for supposedly flirting with a white woman, received extensive press coverage throughout the country, especially a month later, when the two men who were arrested—the woman's husband and his half brother—were found not guilty by an all-white jury. According to the *New York Times,* "The jury acquitted the defendants after deliberating for just 67 minutes—and only that long, one of them said afterward, because they stopped to have a soda pop in order to stretch things out and 'make it look good.'"[38]

Rosa Parks thought the murder of Emmett Till paralleled "an incident that had happened in Montgomery not too long before . . . except this was a young [black] minister who . . . was supposed to have done something."[39] A short while later, she says, "Some men took him out to the Alabama River on a bridge, and he supposedly jumped over into the river. . . . They told his mother she had better keep quiet about it, which she did." The national press ignored that case, according to Rosa, because it was all local people, but as secretary of the Montgomery branch of the NAACP, "I knew it well." She added that many other cases came to "my attention that nothing came out of because the persons who were abused would be too intimidated to sign an affidavit or to make a statement."

Rosa Parks was not intimidated on December 1, 1955, agreeing to challenge bus segregation in court, and neither were some others. Fred Gray returned to Montgomery on that Thursday night and met with three people: Rosa Parks, Ed Nixon, and Jo Ann Robinson. Parks retained him as her attorney, Nixon outlined the strategy, and Robinson prepared the bus boycott. Jo Ann was a professor of English at Alabama State College, which is where she and Fred met, but her passion was the Women's Political Council (WPC) of Montgomery, a middle-class black organization dedicated to improving the status of African Americans. Professor Robinson was its president. She carried a special grudge against the Montgomery bus company ever since a driver had kicked her off for sitting too close to the front, an embarrassment that made her blush every time she told the story. The WPC had drawn up plans for a one-day bus boycott years earlier, according to Robinson, and then had been prepared to go forward with Claudette Colvin. She did not want to be disappointed again, so as soon as Fred Gray confirmed that Rosa Parks had committed to battle, and that Ed Nixon had given his blessing, Robinson went to work.[40]

Jo Ann recalled: "I didn't go to bed that night," instead she went to Alabama State and used a mimeograph machine to make thirty-five thousand copies of a flyer urging blacks to boycott city buses on the day of Parks's trial.[41] The flyer read, in part, "Don't ride the bus to work, to town, or any place on Monday, December 5. Another Negro woman has been arrested and put in jail because she refused to give up her bus seat. . . . If you work, take a cab, or share a ride, or walk."[42] On Friday, Robinson called

Nixon at three in the morning, just to make sure he was not sleeping and to describe her plans to deputize two of her students to distribute the flyers to local churches, bars, and barbershops, the social media of the twentieth century.[43]

Robinson's initiative pleased Nixon, but he wanted to leave little to chance, especially since he had to work as a porter that weekend. He worried whether blacks would join the fight, a dangerous battle with an uncertain outcome at best, and thought that pastors at the local churches could influence their parishioners to participate. Nixon had a list of eighteen preachers tacked on the wall of his den, and he started to call them at five o'clock that morning. He wanted all to join the effort, but one, in particular, intrigued him.

Atlanta-born Dr. Martin Luther King Jr., with a newly minted doctorate from Boston University, was a twenty-six-year-old newcomer to Montgomery, unknown nationally, but the most dynamic speaker Nixon had ever heard. Watching the new pastor of the Dexter Avenue Baptist Church speak at an NAACP conference in August, Nixon had told a fellow audience member, "You know, that guy made a heck of a good talker. . . . I don't know how I'm going do it, but one of these days, I'm gonna hang him to the stars."[44]

He called King on Friday morning, December 2, asked if he would back the boycott from the pulpit, but MLK hesitated, perhaps because he was still new to the community, and asked E.D. to call back. When Nixon finished his round of calls and returned to King, the young preacher agreed, and E.D. smiled into the phone, "I'm glad of that Reverend King, 'cause I already talked to eighteen other people [and] told them to meet at your church this evening."[45]

Ed Nixon had one more move on the chessboard, perhaps the

most important. He worried that many blacks might miss the call to boycott, despite the leaflets and the preachers. Nixon needed a bigger megaphone, so he called Joe Azbell, a white reporter he knew at the *Montgomery Advertiser*, the city's largest newspaper, and met him at Union Station with a copy of the handbill.[46] Nixon wanted a story to run on the front page of Sunday's paper to publicize the boycott, and Azbell, the city editor, had the necessary clout. The *Montgomery Advertiser* had not been especially sensitive to the black community, but Azbell recognized a scoop and promised to do his best.

Nixon had done all he could to ensure the boycott's success, but before leaving on his Pullman run, he made a final telephone call to Johnnie Carr, Rosa Parks's girlhood friend. Nixon had been president of the NAACP when Carr's membership in the organization encouraged Rosa to join. She had experienced all the disappointments, shared Parks's perspective, and deserved to hear progress. She remembered Nixon's words: "Mrs. Carr, they've arrested the wrong woman now."[47] It was an understatement.

The front page of Sunday's *Montgomery Advertiser* carried a headline above the fold that read as though E.D. himself had written it: "Negro Groups Ready Boycott of City Lines."[48] The opening words of Azbell's article made it sound like a covert CIA operation: "A 'top-secret' meeting of Montgomery Negroes who plan a boycott of city buses Monday is scheduled at 7 pm Monday at the Holt Street Baptist Church for 'further instructions' in an 'economic reprisal' campaign against segregation on city buses."[49] Nixon had returned to Montgomery Sunday morning, saw the paper, and called the ministers to offer encouragement: "Have you read the paper this morning? . . . Read it. Take it to church with you. . . . Tell the peoples [*sic*] what is happening."

And then he added a numerical objective: "Tell them that we want . . . two thousand people at Holt Street Baptist Church tomorrow night for the purpose of letting the folks know that we aren't gonna take this laying down no longer."[50] According to Martin Luther King, the article had "a greater impetus for the success of the boycott than anything before."[51]

E.D. resembled an amateur dart player, missing his target by a wide margin. That Monday night, five thousand, not two thousand, people packed the church "to its outer doors," according to the *Montgomery Advertiser,* spilling over into surrounding streets "and blocking traffic."[52] Fred Gray, who had spent the morning in court with Rosa Parks, pleading not guilty and paying a $14 fine, recalled: "I arrived at Holt Street Baptist Church about six . . . only to find that I could not get a parking space within three blocks of the church."[53] The gathering that evening looked like the turnout for a rock concert, and reflected the overwhelming participation in the day's bus protest. The press reported that "eighty or ninety percent of the Negroes who normally used the buses joined the boycott."[54] People walked, rode together in black-owned taxis that agreed to charge the same ten-cent fare as the buses, and then they walked some more. After seeing the crowd, Nixon suspected that those few blacks on the buses on December 5 had not heard about the boycott. He summed up: "We surprised ourselves."[55]

The show of support for Rosa Parks succeeded, but nothing would change without follow-through. Earlier in the day, Fred Gray; Ed Nixon; Reverend Ralph Abernathy, who was minister of the First Baptist Church; and a few other leaders, formed a new organization called the Montgomery Improvement Association to manage the protest. They planned to address the gathering at the church that evening, and elected Reverend Martin Luther King as president. According to Nixon, King became president because he was a newcomer: "He had not been here long enough for the city fathers to put their hand on him. Usually, they find some young man come to town, and they . . . pat him on the shoulder, tell him what a nice church he got . . . [and] his mouth is closed forever."[56] No one could silence a living and breathing Martin Luther King, and the young preacher would make the most of the floodlights.

Rosa Parks received a standing ovation from the crowd at the Holt Street Baptist Church, the applause echoing like rumbling thunder, but she left the talking to others. Ed Nixon warned the assembled, "You who are afraid, you better get your hat and coat and go home. This is going to be a long and drawn-out affair."[57] Those words proved prophetic, but King stole the show in his talk, first with a bow to Rosa Parks: "Since it had to happen, I'm happy that it happened to a person like Mrs. Parks, for nobody can doubt the boundless outreach of her integrity. Nobody can doubt the height of her character, [and] nobody can doubt the depth of her Christian commitment."[58] Second, King made a plea for nonviolent protest: "There comes a time, my friends, when people get tired of being plunged across the abyss of humiliation, where they experience the bleakness of nagging despair. There comes a time when people get tired of being pushed out of the glittering sunlight. . . . We are here this evening because we're tired now. And I want to say that we are not here advocating violence. We have never done that. . . . We believe in the Christian religion. . . . The only weapon that we have in our hands this evening is the weapon of protest."

Before the meeting ended, Reverend Abernathy translated King's poetry into action, and proposed, on behalf of the leadership of the Montgomery Improvement Association, a code of conduct until the discriminatory treatment stopped. "First, that the citizens of Montgomery . . . refrain from riding buses owned and operated in the city of Montgomery; second, that every person owning . . . an automobile will use [them] in assisting other persons to get to work without charge; and three, that the employers . . . afford transportation for your own employees."[59] He asked those sitting in the church who agreed to please rise. Rosa watched the audience from the platform, hoping for signs of approval, and recalled, "People started getting up, one or two at a time at first, and then more and more, until every single person in that church was standing, and outside the crowd was cheering 'Yes!'"[60]

She smiled, knowing her grandfather would approve.

The battle took longer than anyone expected and became violent. On Thursday, December 8, the fourth day of the boycott, representatives of the Montgomery Improvement Association, including King, Nixon, and Jo Ann Robinson, met with bus company officials to compromise, proposing that blacks be "hired as drivers on routes heavily patronized by Negroes and that seats on buses be put on a 'first come, first served' basis."[61] Martin Luther King sounded like the Neville Chamberlain of civil rights by saying at the meeting, "We are not trying to change the segregation laws. But we are trying to peacefully arrange better accommodations for Negroes." In a grand miscalculation, attorneys for the bus company rejected these modest proposals as violating state law requiring separate seating for whites and blacks, turning what might have been a minor skirmish for respectability into an all-out war for desegregation.

The Montgomery Improvement Association planned for a long siege, with transportation logistics worthy of study at West Point. King disclosed a network of "108 cab drivers, a private car pool of 200, and eight filling station proprietors who are giving special discounts to auto owners transporting persons who are participating in the boycott."[62] That network would help blacks stay off the buses indefinitely and would cost the bus company an estimated $3,000 in revenue per day—more than half its daily income. By the end of December, the boycott had gained strength. According to King, "Where you used to find one or two colored passengers on the buses, you'll have to look for hours to find one today."[63] He was proud of the black community: "The colored citizens of this town have united like never before. I have never seen anything like it."[64]

The boycott forced the bus company to raise fares by 50 percent in the middle of January 1956 to try to balance its books.[65] The increased cost, borne entirely by the remaining white riders, angered Mayor William Gayle, who told the police to start a get-tough ticketing program to break the black transportation system.[66] One of the first victims of this unfriendly campaign was Reverend King himself, arrested on Monday, January 30 for allegedly driving thirty miles an hour in a twenty-five-mile-an-hour zone. King, denying the charge, said he had pulled up at McDonald and Monroe Streets, a busy pick-up point in the ride-sharing network, and overheard a police officer in a parked patrol car say to his partner, "There is that King fellow."[67] King may have tried to ease the tension by omitting a few expletives from the officer's comments, but after his release that evening, a bomb exploded in the front yard of his house. MLK was not home, and no one was injured, although his wife, Coretta, and their seven-week-old baby were shaken by the blast, which damaged the concrete front porch. Two nights later, a bomb exploded on the front lawn of Ed Nixon's home, again leaving no injuries but delivering a loud message.[68] MLK told the press that the city had embarked on a two-point program: "First, a campaign of intimidation through a series of harassing arrests to . . . tear down our morale. Secondly, they are attempting to provoke violence."[69] He would not let them succeed on either count.

Bombs were not the only weapons of mass intimidation. The Montgomery Fair Department Store fired Rosa Parks on Saturday, January 7, 1956, and Raymond lost his barber chair at nearby Maxwell Air Force Base when many of his former white customers drifted away.[70] Neither of them could find other employment in Montgomery. Rosa recalled harassing telephone calls that began soon after her arrest and never stopped. "There were people who called to say that I should be beaten or killed because I was causing so much trouble."[71] Rosa and Raymond suffered for triggering the protest, and so did others who worked for the boycott. Private car owners in the ride-sharing program found their tires slashed, gas tanks filled with sugar, or both.

Few succumbed to the pressure, thanks to an extensive support network. Georgia Gilmore, who had been a midwife but became a cook to help feed the tired walkers, explained: "I made the pies. I made full meals. I'd have two meats every day. I'd have chicken, maybe meat loaf with cream potatoes, cheese and macaroni, rutabagas, peas with okra, lettuce and tomato, apple pie, and iced tea. We were walking . . . but we weren't hungry."[72] She had been insulted by a bus driver once but softened somewhat when reflecting back on the boycott: "Oh, it wasn't so bad, really. You'd get cussed at now and then. They'd holler out the window, 'N——r, don't you know it's better to ride than walk?' We'd say under our breath, 'No, cracker. I ain't gettin' on till Jim Crow gets off.'"

The boycott ended Friday, December 21, 1956, more than a year after it started, when the U.S. Supreme Court's order banning segregation on buses went into effect.[73] The *New York Times* marked the occasion with a front-page story about a meeting among blacks celebrating the decision: "A boycott leader, the Rev. Martin Luther King Jr., urged the gathering to patronize the buses, but warned against violence."[74] The yearlong battle had transformed the charismatic local preacher into a national figure, but others deserve credit for the victory, not least Rosa Parks, who started it all. Ed Nixon exaggerated when he said, "If Mrs. Parks had gotten up and given that cracker his seat, you'd never heard of Reverend King," but she surely sparked his debut with her sacrifice.[75] For her part, Rosa Parks shunned the spotlight and gave credit to MLK: "I am not an absolute supporter of nonviolence in all situations. But I strongly believe that the civil rights movement of the 1950s and 1960s could never have been so successful without Dr. King and his firm belief in nonviolence."[76]

A little more than a year before he was murdered in Memphis in 1968 by a white racist named James Earl Ray, King offered a formula for avoiding armed revolution: "Riots grow out of intolerable conditions. Violent revolts are generated by revolting conditions, and there is nothing more dangerous than to build a society with a large segment of people who feel they have no stake in it; who feel they have nothing to lose."[77] That same sentiment had pushed Rosa Parks to gamble everything to fight Jim Crow, but she did it peacefully, with Martin Luther King's guidance. When she died at ninety-two on October 24, 2005, Democratic senator Harry Reid of Nevada issued the following statement: "Rosa Parks's bravery triggered the Montgomery bus boycott. The boycott gained national attention, ushered an atmosphere of change, and was the precursor to landmark legislation such as the Civil Rights Act and the Voting Rights Act."[78]

An impressive legacy.

CHAPTER 6

MEDICAL CRISES
AND PANDEMICS

I n April 2020 President Donald Trump touted hydroxychloro-
quine, a drug approved to treat malaria, lupus, and rheuma-
toid arthritis, as a potential game changer in the battle against
COVID-19, despite a warning from Dr. Anthony Fauci, director
of the National Institute of Allergy and Infectious Diseases, that
it was unproven. But the president persisted, giving advice to those
stricken with disease: "If you wanted, you can have a prescription. You get a prescription. You know the expression, what the
hell do you have to lose?"[1]

Patients with life-threatening illnesses often try experimental
cures, and few would blame them, but the president of the United
States blundered by encouraging such a Hail Mary approach to
medical therapy. Trump erred not only because hydroxychloro-
quine was found to be ineffective against the virus and potentially harmful, but, more broadly, because the chief executive has
a wider constituency. Dramatic treatments in otherwise hopeless
cases bring money and medical talent to a narrow cause, as doctors and drug companies respond to desperate pleas. But society may be better off using scarce medical resources to promote

programs with a larger footprint, such as searching for new anti-biotics. The headlines given experimental cures for fatal diseases described below crowd out less spectacular work, such as finding an antidote for the seasonal flu or preparing for a pandemic. The federal government must promote those projects, called public goods, just like it provides for national defense, national parks, and clean air—because no one else will. It may also mean restricting access to unproven drugs and speculative medical procedures, sacrificing a life to improve the greater good. Think of it as triage in the battlefield, an unpopular but necessary strategy with limited resources. Good medical talent is always scarce.

D octors often encourage patients to try the untried when all else fails, even though the U.S. Food and Drug Administration (FDA) restricts access to pharmaceutical trials. FDA officials worry that excessively easy access to experimental drugs, for example, could stifle the development of new treatments by shrinking the pool of patients available for rigorously designed, scientific clinical trials. But no physician wants to deny the sick a potential cure. Howard Fine, former chief of the Neuro-Oncology Branch at the National Cancer Institute, said he received calls from parents of dying children, pleading, "Just give me this drug. What have we got to lose?"[2] Fine saw two thousand to three thousand brain tumor patients a year, knew that the "vast majority" will die within twelve months, and said, while emphasizing this is not an official opinion, "Ethically speaking, who has the right to say to a patient, 'You have no right to try this medicine even though you're dying?'" Some worry that offering terminal cancer patients unproven therapies preys on their desperation, but as John Harris, a professor of bioethics at England's

University of Manchester, put it, "How can you lower the bar too much for people who are going to die anyway and for whom this is a last hope?"[3]

Some physicians have taken matters into their own hands and experimented on themselves.[4] Peter Baginsky, bald and bespectacled, sixty-four years old, and a diabetes specialist from Forestville, California, had already beaten the odds, surviving five years after surgery in January 2009 to remove a glioblastoma, the same type of aggressive brain cancer that killed Senator Ted Kennedy in thirteen months. When the cancer returned in January 2014, "I was very depressed,"[5] he said, but Baginsky had one hope: an experimental approach in Zurich, Switzerland, using a focused-ultrasound treatment to burn a hole through the inch-long tumor deep in his brain. The six-hour procedure would be supervised by three neurosurgeons, without charge, but the hospital care and other services would come to $22,000, plus travel expenses. Baginsky explained his decision, "I had nothing to lose, actually. Just a lot of money, but everything to gain."[6]

Baginsky, who studied English literature as an undergraduate at Harvard University, served in the Peace Corps after college, and then went to Harvard Medical School, understood this was a long shot.[7] He traveled with his wife, Cheryl Hanson, to Zurich, and on Tuesday, March 4, 2014, survived the ordeal with no pain, although he said that his head felt "almost unbearably hot" during the procedure. The neurosurgeons monitored him for a week in the hospital, were satisfied there were no adverse side effects, and considered the safe outcome a success. The press reported that the "Focused Ultrasound Foundation, based in Virginia, called it a 'key landmark event' in the evolution of ultrasound as a non-invasive treatment for brain cancer, an alternative to surgery and radiation."[8] It was an overstatement. Peter Baginsky died on

Friday, November 14, 2014, nine months after the procedure, surrounded by his wife, daughter, and son.[9] In December 2018 the U.S. Food and Drug Administration approved ultrasound to treat Parkinson's disease, but not brain cancer.[10]

High-profile patients seeking novel treatments with little chance of success encourages experimentation. On Wednesday, March 6, 2019, Alex Trebek, the longtime host of the TV game show *Jeopardy!*, announced that he had been diagnosed with stage four pancreatic cancer. A still-spry seventy-eight years old, but with a deeply furrowed brow framed by a full head of grey hair, Trebek said candidly, "The prognosis for this is not very encouraging, but I'm going to fight this, and I'm going to keep working. I plan to beat the low survival rate statistics for this disease."[11] He then tried to lighten the mood, as though chatting with one of the show's contestants: "Truth told, I have to! Because under the terms of my contract, I have to host *Jeopardy!* for three more years! So help me. Keep the faith, and we'll win."

Watching Alex Trebek on *Jeopardy!* had become a nightly ritual for more than twenty million viewers. Ken Jennings, the winningest player on the program, compared Trebek's trusted voice to that of former CBS news anchor Walter Cronkite, but Alex added a wry sense of humor. During an episode of Tournament of Champions, bringing back former *Jeopardy!* winners, Trebek emerged from backstage to open the show wearing a jacket, dress shirt, tie—but without trousers. The three contestants, including Jennings, had proposed the relaxed attire to ease the tension, but only Alex kept his promise.[12] He was less playful nine months after his cancer diagnosis. Trebek had enjoyed a near remission at first, buoying his hopes, but the disease returned, and the battle escalated. He said: "We may try a new protocol, a different chemo or something in the trial stage that is not chemotherapy. I don't mind experimenting . . . so let's go for it."[13] Alex Trebek died at age eighty on November 8, 2020.

Experimental treatments often take time to succeed, so they are given considerable support even if they monopolize scarce medical talent. In 1967 Louis Washkansky, a fifty-five-year-old man from Cape Town with a failing heart, underwent the first successful human heart transplant, an operation conducted by South African cardiac surgeon Dr. Christiaan Barnard, assisted by thirty physicians. Washkansky survived only eighteen days, but fifty-plus years later, more than five thousand heart transplants are performed annually throughout the world, and patients live an average of twelve years.[14]

John Bogle, founder of the Vanguard family of mutual funds, born with a heart defect called arrhythmogenic right ventricular dysplasia, suffered his first heart attack when he was just thirty-one years old and had at least five others after that. In October 1995, at age sixty-six, he entered Philadelphia's Hahnemann University Hospital to await a heart transplant.[15] Bogle worried as soon as he got there: "By that time," he recalled, "my heart was about to give out. . . . I was trying to find a heart transplant and was taken into the heart transplant system in which you are basically dated when you get in there; there's no favoritism. And you get in line and wait, and I waited . . . being kept alive on intravenous."[16]

Bogle admitted that he had second thoughts while waiting: "During that time, I started to think pretty seriously about, you know, whether an old guy if you will, should get a heart destined for a younger person. And I finally decided that the system was the system, and maybe I could be of some use as a citizen and as a human being to the world."

Exactly twenty-one years after the operation, on Tuesday, February 21, 2017, Bogle gathered with his surgeons, Rohinton Morris and Louis Samuels, to reminisce along with their staff.[17] Jack recalled waiting 128 days in the hospital before they transferred the donated heart of a thirty-year-old into his chest cavity. "I was pushing the limit of transplant age," he acknowledged, then added, "Now, I'm trying to be a superager. I'm pushing eighty-eight and hope to push to eighty-nine." Dr. Morris, a great surgeon, knew how to flatter his patient, and interrupted: "Everyone knows that Jack's index funds have beaten the average mutual fund, but he's also beaten the odds when it comes to his heart." Bogle smiled, knowing that investors had poured more than $300 billion into Vanguard the year before, more than any other mutual fund, but mainly because Morris and Samuels had given him a new lease on life, paying bigger dividends than anyone expected. Jack ended his remarks with a message from his heart, and with a tear in his eye: "I wouldn't have lived to see my dreams realized, and that's been gratifying, what the doctors have done for me."

Medical success stories like the February 21, 1996, heart transplant of John Bogle, who died at eighty-nine on Wednesday, January 16, 2019, of esophageal cancer, encourage fatally ill patients to seek novel treatments, hoping for miraculous results. Abigail Burroughs, a junior at the University of Virginia and a member of the prestigious Jefferson Literary and Debating Society, had been diagnosed in 1999 with squamous cell carcinoma of the head and neck that spread to her tongue.[18] She was treated successfully with surgery, radiation, and chemotherapy at Johns Hopkins Hospital in Baltimore, and had been planning to take a Caribbean cruise with her three best friends, "I definitely know the odds aren't that great," she told a newspaper reporter, "but I refuse to give up."[19]

When the cancer spread to Abigail's lungs in early 2001, her physician, Maura Gillison of Johns Hopkins, noted that initial investigative trials of two then-experimental drugs, not yet approved for use by the FDA, Iressa and C225, had shown promise. "She has no therapeutic options left, so [trying the experimental drugs] is the most reasonable option."[20] But neither London-based AstraZeneca, which made Iressa, nor New York's ImClone Systems, which developed C225, had programs for such cases. An AstraZeneca spokesperson said, "The bottom line is, since we don't have data on Iressa for head and neck cancer, we do not feel we can make it available to her."[21] A petition signed by more than six thousand in the University of Virginia community, a resolution passed by the city council of Falls Church, Virginia, and intervention by the state's U.S. senators, John W. Warner and George Allen Jr., succeeded in reversing the decision, but it was too late.[22] Abigail died in her sleep on Saturday, June 9, 2001, at her Falls Church home.[23] Abigail's father, Frank Burroughs, had said before she died, "She wishes she could write everybody a letter and thank them for what they've done on her behalf."[24]

Most doctors cannot resist trying to extend life, even with limited benefits. A nurse commented in a survey published in the *Journal of Critical Care* that a "physician views it as a personal failure if the patient doesn't live."[25] Dr. Gillison, who had given Abigail nine months to live, said of the experimental treatment, "Perhaps it could have prolonged her period of life."[26] A cardiologist explained that one of the challenges for a doctor treating seriously ill patients is "not wanting to let them down, particularly when you start out being able to promise a lot, and usually you can."[27] A surgical consultant added, "I think most surgeons see that if there's a small chance, then you've got nothing to lose, and you give it a try. . . . There's always scope to . . . get a result which is better than death." But an article in the *Journal of Medical Ethics,* titled, "Reasons Doctors Provide Futile Treatment at the End of Life," took a harsher view. It asked physicians to justify their behavior, which, though compassionate, "wastes scarce health care resources."

The critically ill want hope, so every doctor pushes the boundary, but someone has to worry about the greater good—a broader perspective beyond an individual patient—and failure to do so brings collateral damage. For example, a study at an academically affiliated hospital examined the *opportunity cost* of futile treatments in the intensive care unit. Skilled physicians tending to a patient with no prospect of recovery means delayed treatment for others in the queue. The study measured those costs and concluded, "It is unjust when a patient is unable to access intensive care because ICU beds are occupied by patients who cannot benefit from such care."[28] The analysis suggested further that ignoring opportunity cost "is not only inefficient and wasteful, but it is also contrary to Medicine's responsibility to apply health care resources to best serve society." Individual physicians do not focus on allocating medical services, nor should they, but Congress and the president should, including providing for low-probability events such as a pandemic.

Covid-19 caught America unprepared, despite having been warned. The *New England Journal of Medicine* (*NEJM*), founded more than two hundred years ago, is the most prestigious publication in the medical world. Each week, it delivers to six hundred thousand subscribers peer-reviewed articles on medical science and clinical practice that expose readers to promising new treatment options and medical breakthroughs. It is the Bible of health care professionals. The March 31, 2016, issue contained a report, "The Neglected Dimension of Global Security—A Framework for Countering Infectious-Disease Crises," that should have alerted the world to the danger of an influenza pandemic.[29]

The study, chaired by Peter Sands of Harvard University's Kennedy School, and staffed by the National Academy of Medicine, began by referencing the Spanish flu of 1918, and delivered a warning worthy of the prophet Jeremiah: "Infectious disease outbreaks that turn into epidemics and potential pandemics can cause massive loss of life and huge economic disruption."[30] But that was just the opening thunder. The article proposed "greater investment in countering infectious disease threats," and put that recommendation into a military framework: "Potential pandemics should be considered not just as important health risks but as major threats to the global economy and global security."[31]

Advocating a call to arms against pandemics should have hit newspaper front pages during the 2016 election year, but it barely made the small print in the business section.[32] Peter Sands and his coauthors probably were unhappy, though not surprised, for as they wrote in their paper: "The private sector foresees relatively little return on such investments."[33] But this is where the government should act, using general tax revenues to finance public goods such as infectious disease control. The problem with pandemics is their rarity, so "Governments find it difficult to justify spending money on avoiding relatively low-probability crises." Former U.S. Treasury secretary Lawrence Summers said, "This is an area where the urgent has crowded out the profoundly important. In too many countries, pressing near-term needs and budgetary pressures have prevented the establishment of necessary infrastructures for public health."[34] Pandemics fall into a black hole between public and private enterprise, with no one to shoulder the bill. As a result, the Sands report concluded: "Pandemics arguably pose more of a threat to human lives than war, terrorism, or natural disasters. . . . It seems remarkable how little we spend."[35]

A second warning came in September 2019, three months before COVID-19 spread like a medieval epidemic, when the Council of Economic Advisers (CEA)—a tiny agency buried in Donald Trump's Executive Office of the President, with fewer than one hundred professionals on staff—issued a remarkable report: *Mitigating the Impact of Pandemic Influenza Through Vaccine Innovation*.[36] The forty-page study built on the insight of the *New England Journal of Medicine* article, explaining that private companies underinvest because the last serious pandemic "occurred a hundred years ago [and] may lead consumers and insurers to underestimate the probability and potential impact of a future influenza pandemic."[37] The CEA report added a subtle twist, maintaining that private companies "cannot capture the insurance value" of a vaccine, which benefits society by making people feel more secure "even if the pandemic does not occur."[38] The authors concluded by recommending that the government "partner with the private sector to develop and adopt new vaccine technologies that mitigate the risks of pandemic influenza."[39]

Congress passed the Employment Act of 1946 establishing the Council of Economic Advisers, and directed the CEA to "develop and recommend to the president . . . policies to foster and promote free competitive enterprise, to avoid economic fluctuations . . . and to maintain employment, production, and purchasing power."[40] Donald Trump's CEA did more than that in its special report, describing in prophetic detail the potential damage of failure to prepare: "In a severe pandemic, healthy people might avoid work and normal social interactions in an attempt to avert illness by limiting contact with sick persons. By incapacitating a large fraction of the population, including individuals who work in critical infrastructure and defense sectors, pandemic influenza could threaten U.S. national security."[41]

The CEA's crystal ball described the upheaval six months before it happened.

Proper follow-up to the warnings might have prevented the massive disruption from COVID-19.[42] Physicians prefer to extend patients' lives, even for a few months, rather than work on pandemic control, a rare but catastrophic event. Dr. Reuel Stallones, the founding dean of the University of Texas School of Public Health, once said, "Epidemiology ranks low in the hierarchy—in the pecking order, the rewards system. Yet it holds the key to reducing lots of human suffering."[43] He was right. According to an article published in the *Journal of the American Medical Association* (*JAMA*), "Of all the resource-shortage crises this nation is expected to confront in the future, the problem of resource distribution is likely to be most acute and problematic in medicine."[44] President Trump should have followed the recommendations of his advisers to mitigate the potential damage of a pandemic. It is a public good, worthy of the chief executive's attention, and far more valuable than offering dubious medical advice after the fact.

Preparing a vaccine for the novel coronavirus would have been scientifically impossible beforehand, but stockpiling ventilators, surgical masks, and face shields would have been easy.[45] The president could have asked Congress for funds to build storage facilities for personal protective equipment throughout the United States, similar to the nuclear silos that dot the countryside (but a lot cheaper). Those storage facilities would have been embarrassing without a pandemic, but certainly less embarrassing than importing masks from China after the tsunami struck.

It is time to prepare for the next one.

PART III

MAN-MADE DISASTERS

PART II

HUMAN-MADE DISASTERS

CHAPTER 7

ROGUE TRADERS

Zac Rankin, a senior at Southeast Missouri State University in Cape Girardeau, Missouri, was captain of the team that won the 2015 stock market contest for college students sponsored by TD Ameritrade, a brokerage firm with more than ten million customers.[1] Rankin led a group of four students to victory over 475 other teams, including those from the Ivy League and from business schools around the country. The group from Southeast Missouri won by turning $500,000 into $1.3 million in a month for a gain of 160 percent, the largest return over that period among all contestants. None of Rankin's teammates were finance majors, but they used the fictitious allocation of a half million dollars as though they were experts in the complicated mathematics of financial options. Rankin said the team recognized quickly that "We had nothing to lose. If we end up losing all five hundred thousand dollars, oh well. We basically just decided to be as risky as possible."[2]

The go-for-broke approach by Rankin and his teammates, Chelsey Winsor, Ben Asselmeier, and John Racanelli, relied on the structure of the Ameritrade stock market game. They understood that the contest rewarded only the biggest gain, while all losses, no matter how large, turned into tiny zeroes. A $1 billion loss meant as little as a $10 drop. Rankin and Company won by ignoring safe investments—an appropriate strategy under the circumstances—crowning each of the Missouri students a Warren Buffett lookalike. That same concept of downside protection gives real-life securities traders at banks the incentive to ignore losses, and the damage from the failure to monitor them burdens taxpayers with costly bailouts.

In July 1992 Nicholas Leeson, a stocky twenty-five-year-old, stepped into the trading room of the Singapore International Monetary Exchange (Simex) for the first time.[3] He heard traders shouting as if at a championship boxing match, trying to profit by buying and selling futures contracts on the Nikkei stock index, the Dow Jones of the Japanese stock market. He had been working at Baring Investment Bank for three years, waiting for the opportunity to trade—a physical activity back then—with the chance to make it big. He recalled, "I could smell and see the money."[4] Nick, who stayed in Singapore until 1995, did not know he would lose more than he could ever spend and, in the process, destroy Barings, the blue-blood British bank, founded in 1762, that had helped Thomas Jefferson finance the Louisiana Purchase in the nineteenth century and managed Queen Elizabeth II's personal fortune in the twentieth.

Nick had come from the working-class community of Watford, England, where his mother was a nurse and his father a plasterer. Most of his friends had gone into the building trades as plumbers, electricians, and carpenters, but his mother had encouraged a wider landscape when he began looking for his first job in 1985. Nick remembered that she typed his application to Coutts & Co., a private bank and wealth manager, and when he landed the position in London, despite average grades and failing his math exams, she sent him to work every day with "ironed shirts and polished shoes."[5] She had already paved a path for Nick when she died two years later, but his two sisters, aged thirteen and ten, were left rudderless. He made a promise to her memory: "I would look after the family. I'd do anything to help the girls along." When he began to trade for Barings, he expected to fulfill that promise, knowing that becoming a trader "was the way to earn a fortune and buy a Porsche."

Nick Leeson had learned a craft before arriving at Barings. He left Coutts in 1987 and moved to the London branch of Morgan Stanley, an American investment bank, where he apprenticed in the complicated world of futures and options, including confirming transactions of traders who used the bank's capital hoping to make money. He knew that settling trades, called back-office operations, was about as glamorous as managing equipment for a soccer team, but sending cash daily from losers to winners kept everyone honest. It was tedious work that tracked the profits and losses of brokerage firms. But he also knew that his "friends in Watford would have been amazed" to learn that he earned a salary of £20,000, a lot by their standards.[6] And Leeson understood from transferring millions between buyers and sellers that the big money lay in trading, so when a friend offered him a job at Baring Bank in 1989 and promised a shot at becoming a trader, he jumped at the opportunity, even though he took a £5,000 pay cut. Nick waited three years for the right opportunity, volunteering to go to Singapore when Barings opened an office there to transact for its customers on Simex. The bank put Nick in charge of back-office operations, because of his expertise, and made him a trader, because of his passion—a combination as explosive as dynamite.

Barings had escaped a near catastrophe a century earlier, and like most missteps, it began in triumph. In 1886 the company, led by Edmund "Ned" Baring, recently crowned Lord Revelstoke, managed the flotation of shares in Guinness, the Irish brewer, on the London Stock Exchange. The lucky few investors allocated stock by Barings in the public offering earned profits of more than 50 percent on the first day of trading, making the Barings name synonymous with instant wealth. The feat further burnished the investment company's reputation for financing savvy, lauded earlier in the nineteenth century by the French statesman the Duc de Richelieu: "There are six great powers in Europe: England, France, Russia, Austria, Prussia, and the Baring Brothers."[7] Ned Baring tripped over his press clippings.

In 1890 Barings underwrote a £2 million issue of the Buenos Aires Water Supply and Drainage Company, a utility in the emerging market of Argentina.[8] In most underwritings, an investment company such as Barings, often called a merchant bank in Europe, presells the securities before advancing the funds to the issuer, in this case the Argentinian water company, avoiding losses and pocketing the price difference, called an underwriting fee, for its marketing services. But flush from his Guinness victory, Ned Baring advanced the £2 million to the South American utility and held the shares, speculating on a price increase rather than preselling the securities to customers and earning the relatively small underwriting fee. He would have been a hero had the Buenos Aires shares soared in value like those of the Irish brewery, but South America disappointed, as it often has since, the securities collapsed in price, and the losing gamble overwhelmed Baring Brothers' capital. Threatened with bankruptcy, Barings partners ran to the Bank of England for help, and in a preview of the modern "too big to fail," the Bank arranged for a bailout that saved the company.[9] The episode restrained Baring Brothers in the twentieth century but conferred a sense of entitlement to rescue that may have contributed to its ultimate demise.

A trader such as Nick Leeson wears a number of hats piled on his head, requiring a balancing act to prevent them from toppling to the trading floor. His main job was to execute orders on Simex for Barings' clients, buying or selling Nikkei stock index futures according to customer instructions. Barings earned a commission for completing these orders, similar to a real estate broker's fee for selling a house, an activity that bored Leeson. He knew that the real money came from proprietary trading, a fancy term for speculation, buying or selling Nikkei stock futures for the company's account and betting on whether prices would rise or fall. Most investment banks, including Barings, allowed some of its traders to combine customer business with speculation, but within limits to avoid big losses. An undisciplined speculator, like Ned Baring a century earlier, could threaten the firm's existence.

Leeson began to speculate as soon as he started on Simex in July 1992, attracted by a year-end bonus for profitability.[10] A bonus of £150,000 on top of a £50,000 salary, a realistic prospect, could buy a Porsche with something left over for an intimate party.[11] He said later, "Toward the end of the year, bonuses were all anyone talked about."[12] Nick also knew that bonuses can at worst decline to zero but could not become negative because traders never had to repay the bank for losses. He could get fired for losing too much, of course, but, then, he would just start over at another bank with a clean slate, like so many others he knew. The bonus structure of trader compensation, limited downside to keep traders from jumping ship with unlimited upside for big profits, created a skewed payoff and encouraged gambling, just like the TD Ameritrade stock contest. Nick never said he "decided to be as risky as possible," like Zac Rankin and his Southeast Missouri teammates, because Barings' managers would have pulled his trading privileges. But he shared the collegians' attitude when booking losses: "It wasn't our money, and it was not our clients' money, it was Barings' money."[13]

Barings understood these dangerous incentives, just like every other bank, and monitored its traders, especially freshmen like Leeson, to curb reckless behavior. Ron Baker, a veteran of the Bankers Trust Company, an American bank with a history of trading expertise, was one of Leeson's bosses who, instead of restraining Nick, fell victim to his seduction. Leeson promised steady profits by taking advantage of Barings' presence on both Simex and Japan's Osaka Stock Exchange. The Nikkei stock futures traded in both locations, often at slightly different prices because of local imbalances between buyers and sellers, allowing Leeson to arbitrage the two markets. For example, he might buy the Nikkei cheap on Osaka and immediately sell at a higher price on Simex, to capture the difference.[14] Those transactions produced only small profits because prices never deviated by much, but, with patience and persistence, they added up.

Barings' senior management had little background in the new-fangled world of stock index futures, but it could easily understand the principle of arbitrage, an ageless concept that had enriched London bankers as far back as the seventeenth century.[15] Barings' profits grew with Leeson's trading, and the bank's chairman, Peter Baring, met with Brian Quinn, executive director of bank supervision with the Bank of England, the government's monitoring agency of banking activities. Peter described his bank's performance and touted his company's impressive record: "It was not actually terribly difficult to make money in the securities business."[16] His boast was a flashing red light that should have alerted the Bank of England to danger.

Peter Baring, usually a man of few words, made a colossal error of judgment, much like saying that golf is an easy game after a lucky hole in one, all but ensuring a quadruple bogey on the next hole. Nick Leeson almost choked: "Peter Baring should have known better," he contended in a 1996 memoir. "Making money is never easy—his ancestors who built up the bank and took risks and went out to visit canals and railways would never have said that. . . . My father knows that you have to work hard and that you get paid £20 a square yard for plastering, and you've got to keep the customer happy. . . . The laundry on the corner, the boy who delivers newspapers, the lawyer working above the estate agency . . . all know that making money is never easy. And if it's easy, then it's a gamble."[17]

Gambling is what Nick Leeson actually did. He talked arbitrage but was impatient with the nickel-and-dime profits, so he turned to speculation, trying to make a killing. For example, he would buy the Nikkei stock index in Osaka or Simex—whichever was cheaper—just like an arbitrageur. But instead of selling immediately to lock in a profit, he waited, hoping for a price increase, like rolling dice and praying for a seven. Prayer may work in houses of worship, but it loses money in the casino and the stock market, causing anxiety and depression. Nick felt sick when a trade soured as prices declined instead of increasing: "My forehead was beaded with sweat, which I wiped on the cuff of my jacket," he recalled. "A horrible feeling of loss began to creep inside my stomach."

As the losses piled up, Nick only compounded the damage:

"I was winning sometimes, more often I was losing . . . [so I] doubled up the stakes." And he knew the consequences: "This is gambling at its simplest. If you double up, you halve the amount the market needs to turn for you to make your money back." For example, putting $2,000, rather than $1,000, on black at the roulette table makes it easier to win $2,000, but it also doubles the amount you can lose. Nick added, "Everyone knows you shouldn't do it, yet everyone does it."[18] Everyone may do it, but only Nick Leeson could get away with it for almost three years.

Nick had racked up losses of £2 million in 1992 and £24 million the following year—small by later standards, and nothing that would have threatened the existence of Baring Bank, with more than £450 million in capital. But losers do not get bonuses, so Nick turned those losses into profits by covering his tracks in the Singapore back office, where he was in charge as general manager.[19] He hid losses with fake entries in a balance sheet he controlled and also requested cash from Barings' main London office to settle his losing trades, claiming they were margin payments for arbitrage positions. No one in London understood exactly what that meant (any more than you did when reading it just now), but Nick was supposedly making so much money for the bank that few questioned the details.[20] Barings had created the problem by giving traders like Nick a skewed payoff and then compounded the error by putting Leeson in charge of settling his own trades. Nick admitted, "It was a bizarre structure, and one which allowed me to run my own show without anyone interfering."[21]

He almost got caught by an internal Barings audit in mid-1994.[22] Nick's boss, Ron Baker, came to Simex with Ash Lewis, head of internal audit at Barings, who was brought in to check the books. Leeson expected trouble from Lewis: "She had a reputation for absolute thoroughness. . . . I felt as if I were going to be strapped down in a dentist's chair and have my teeth picked over. I was trying to hide one massive hole which she'd spot and dig her metal spike into: 'Aha,' she'd say, cavity in G3.'"[23] Nick must have been brushing his teeth with fluoride because London recalled Lewis before she started, and the subsequent audit found no suspicious entries in the balance sheet, though it did finger the underlying problem: "There is a significant general risk that the controls could be overridden by the general manager. He is the key manager in the front and the back office and can thus initiate transactions on the group's behalf and then ensure that they are settled and recorded according to his own instructions."[24] The audit's final recommendation—that Singapore "should be reorganized so that the general manager is no longer directly responsible for the back office"—might have saved Barings, but nothing was done.[25]

Leeson's cumulative losses ballooned to £164 million at the end of 1994, still not enough to sink Barings, but it forced Nick to redouble his speculations to recoup.[26] He knew it was a gamble: "If you go into any casino in the world, you will see rather grimly determined people sitting at a roulette table doubling up and redoubling when the black goes against them."[27]

John Coffee, a law professor at Columbia University, summarized: "There's no incentive, once you have lost, not to try and double your bet. . . . He's out the door if his losses are detected, so the only rational incentive, from his perspective, is to see if he can, by doubling his bet, turn his loss into a gain."[28]

Leeson's frantic trading brought disaster.[29] On Friday, January 20, 1995, three days after the Kobe earthquake devastated

Japan, he bought a huge position in the Nikkei stock index, betting on economic recovery, and lost more than £100 million over the next two days, almost matching the cumulative loss of the previous two years.[30] In a final spasm of speculation, beginning Monday, February 6, Leeson quadrupled his exposure to the Japanese stock market—similar to buying eight million shares of stock rather than two million—and added positions in other Japanese securities, trying to recover his losses. By Thursday, February 23, 1995, his last day of trading, Leeson's cumulative loss came to more than £800 million—almost double Barings' total capital.[31] He did not show up for work on Friday, leaving a note for his coworkers on the Simex trading floor, saying that he was going to Phuket, Thailand, for his birthday. Nick Leeson would turn twenty-eight on Saturday, February 25, and to celebrate the festive occasion, Barings entered judicial management, similar to Chapter 11 bankruptcy, on Monday, February 27, 1995.[32]

Nick Leeson was a rogue trader, lying about his trading strategy, hiding losses, destroying the company he worked for and the jobs of four thousand employees, but Barings itself shares the blame. Like most banks, its skewed compensation structure encouraged traders to become daredevils, ignoring the fallout. It could have paid its traders more like salesmen on salary, eliminating the asymmetric payoff and sticking to customer business. But Barings wanted the upside of proprietary trading, just like the traders themselves, and chose to monitor them to prevent gambling. And that is where the bank fell woefully short. It put Leeson in charge of Singapore's back office, where he could hide his losses with bogus book entries, an error akin to letting gangster Al Capone, convicted of income tax evasion in 1931, examine his own tax returns. One Barings employee lamented, "The great shame is we're very conservatively run. The one thing we were trying to minimize—proprietary risk taking—is what blew us out of the water."[33]

During 1993 and 1994, senior managers in London ignored the warnings of Leeson's off-the-chart performance, not wanting to ruffle the golden goose's feathers. A Barings executive not directly involved said, "They were very happy with the P&L [profit and loss] Leeson was producing, and they were very defensive when people asked questions."[34] In a postmortem, the Bank of England noted, "Such levels of profitability from so-called 'riskless arbitrage' should have been viewed as abnormal and questionable."[35] Nick said, "My numbers were hopelessly out of orbit, yet nobody stopped me. Although Barings in London discussed what might or might not be going on, for some reason, they let the matter slide."[36]

Many believe that Barings' executives knew of the accumulating losses by December 1994, when they could have been contained, but winked at Leeson's subsequent speculations, hoping they would erase the red ink. Leo Melamed, a former chairman of the Chicago Mercantile Exchange, the largest futures exchange in the world, said, "Once the loss goes to about a hundred million dollars, you figure they would have known about it."[37] Allan Raphael, a portfolio manager at Arnhold and S. Bleichroeder, an investment company with a pedigree almost as old as Barings, said, "It strains the credibility to think that Barings didn't know about this. I don't believe it could be one person."[38] The Bank of England Report, ordered by the House of Commons to explain the mess, confirmed those suspicions: "By January 1995, management of Barings in London became aware of market concerns and rumors regarding the scale of Barings' trading activities. . . .

Barings received a telephone call on January 27, 1995, from the Bank for International Settlements, who had heard rumors to the effect that Barings had margin losses in the Nikkei contract and could not meet its margin calls."[39]

Barings' management suffered from a combination of negligence and wishful thinking, perhaps nurtured by the Bank of England rescue a century earlier. Baring Bank was not "too big to fail" in 1995 but drew comfort from its ancient roots and royal bearing, like a giant spruce, deserving of some protection as a company. Peter Baring, the chairman who had thought it "not actually terribly difficult to make money in the securities business," tried to deflect blame to gain sympathy. He suggested that Leeson led a conspiracy to destroy Barings, believing that a confederate of his had sold short so that "When Barings duly fails . . . [they] will have a wonderful chance to make a profit."[40] The Bank of England found no evidence of conspiracy and refused to save Barings, perhaps to "make an object lesson of the venerable bank," as the *Wall Street Journal* suggested.[41]

Nick Leeson learned the limitation of downside protection as well. In December 1995 a Singapore court sentenced him to six and a half years in prison after he pleaded guilty to "illegally covering up trading losses that led to the collapse of Barings." [42] Judge Richard Magnus imposed a sentence close to the maximum eight years because, he said, "The accused was in a position of trust . . . [and] he had used that position to trade his honesty and integrity. The sentence must be sufficiently substantial to indicate the gravity of the offense to the public." Leeson remained silent during sentencing, standing without expression or tears, but few observers could understand how he expected to get away with covering up losses. Losing money could be forgiven, but every trader knew that hiding losses was an original sin, with banishment from the securities world the minimum punishment. He should have known it would end badly.

Not necessarily.

Howard Rubin was a star mortgage trader at Salomon Brothers, an American investment bank noted for its market power in the 1980s. Howie majored in chemical engineering as an undergraduate at Lafayette College, made money counting cards at Las Vegas blackjack tables, and graduated from Harvard Business School. It was the perfect background for a successful trader, especially the blackjack part, where he bet big only after the odds turned in his favor, similar to a successful trader's artistry. Rubin joined Salomon in 1982 and, in his first two years of trading, earned a record $25 million and $30 million for the firm. He said, "The trading floor at Salomon Brothers felt like a Las Vegas casino. You made your bets, handled the risk, in the midst of a thousand distractions."[43] Lew Ranieri, the Salomon Brothers managing director who invented mortgage-backed securities, called Howie "the most innately talented young trader I have ever seen."

Rubin left Salomon in early 1985 in a dispute over compensation and joined Merrill Lynch, the biggest U.S. retail brokerage firm, trying to build its mortgage trading operation. Merrill gave Howie a three-year contract at $1 million per year, plus a percentage of his trading profits.[44] Merrill's package tripled his Salomon compensation and, more importantly, guaranteed the skewed trader payoff with the promise of an explicit cut of profits. The unlimited upside was like giving Rubin free lottery tickets.

Merrill gave Howard Rubin license to speculate in mortgages because he understood that market and knew how to make money, but in April 1987 Howie went further. He exceeded his authorized trading limits (even stars have them), thinking he would deliver a bonanza. According to a senior Merrill Lynch executive, Rubin thought "he was the world's greatest genius in the mortgage market. He disregarded his superiors as persons who knew nothing. After he proved himself right, he felt he was going to look like a hero."[45] But Rubin lost his bet on mortgage-backed bonds, and instead of cutting his losses like a professional trader, he held the securities without telling anyone, hoping for a recovery. "He just put them in his drawer. We did not know we owned them," said a Merrill manager.[46]

Howie Rubin had lost money before—$45 million in December 1985—and Merrill put him under closer supervision. His trading performance improved but did not prevent the $250 million loss in 1987, the largest in the brokerage industry's history until then. A securities analyst following the company cut Merrill's estimated earnings in half as a result and said, "The question that comes to mind is about their larger controls on the mortgage-backed securities traders. If they hadn't been asleep at the switch, maybe they could have cut their losses."[47] No one explained exactly how Rubin succeeded in hiding trades, but Merrill fired him for the offense and also suspended his immediate boss for failing to monitor him.[48] The company had $3 billion in capital, so Rubin's loss never threatened bankruptcy, but the embarrassment and potential for catastrophe forced the brokerage firm to reorganize. It hired Eugene Rotberg, treasurer of the World Bank, to become an executive vice president, one of only six at Merrill Lynch, with a special mandate "to monitor, manage, and control its risk-taking positions."[49]

The publicity surrounding Merrill's firing of Howard Rubin in April 1987 should have taught traders at banks and brokerage

firms the limitations of their safety net. Nick Leeson should
have learned that losing too much money and compounding the
offense by covering up the red ink leads to unemployment, a
punishment fitting the crime. But in November 1987 the sto-
ryline changed and undermined the lesson. Bear Stearns, another
investment bank looking to tame the mortgage market, gave
Howie Rubin a second chance.[50] The bet paid off a few years later
when Rubin's mortgage group earned $150 million, almost half
of Bear Stearns's record yearly profits. The company's president,
James Cayne, said of Rubin, "He's a superstar."[51] When asked to
comment on Bear Stearns's internal controls and a rumor that
the firm employed "in-house spies" to patrol the corridors to
monitor speculative trades, Cayne said, "We think all people are
honest, but they're more honest if you watch them like a hawk."

Unfortunately for James Cayne, the story did not end there.
In March 2008, financial markets lost confidence in Bear Stearns
as a result of speculative investments—an early episode in the
financial crisis—and investors withdrew funds the company
needed for day-to-day operations, leaving it on the brink of
bankruptcy. In a brokered bailout, the Federal Reserve, America's central bank, arranged for JPMorgan Chase & Co. to buy
Bear Stearns at the flea-market price of $10 per share. The com-
pany had sold for more than $150 a share a year earlier. Many
Bear Stearns executives tried to prevent the loss of confidence
leading to the fire sale, but not James Cayne, who admitted, "I
was playing bridge in Detroit."[52] Alan 'Ace' Greenberg, head of
Bear Stearns before Cayne, said, "In a time of crisis, he flatly
wasn't up to the task."[53]

Taming traders by monitoring, even with X-ray scanning
machines, can never catch the cleverest operatives hiding speculations. They know their business best and can cover their tracks

like a spymaster. Putting traders on straight salary would fix the problem by eliminating the incentive to gamble, but banks resist that simple solution. Companies such as Barings, Bear Stearns, and Merrill Lynch want the upside, just like traders themselves, so they continue to hire financial gunslingers, pay them bonuses for winning big, and hope for the best. The result: taxpayers shoulder costly bailouts when bets go wrong.

CHAPTER 8

ADOLF HITLER AND THE BATTLE OF THE BULGE

Colonel Claus von Stauffenberg, born into an aristocratic German military family, wounded in combat during 1943, and forced to wear a pirate's eye patch, led the July 20, 1944, plan to assassinate Adolf Hitler and end World War II while Germany still had some negotiating power.[1] The thirty-six-year-old colonel placed a bomb-filled briefcase under a thick oak table during a meeting of Nazi leaders in Hitler's Wolf's Lair headquarters, but the timed explosion, which killed four men, failed to hit its target. The fragile conspiracy disintegrated that same day, and reprisals followed immediately. It was not the first attempt on Hitler's life, but the high-level plot, which included senior army officers, stoked Hitler's paranoia and led to two hundred executions, including Stauffenberg.[2]

Hitler requested movies of the tortured hangings, showing bodies twisting from meat hooks, to confirm that his enemies had been punished. He had long suspected the German officer corps of treason, but the July 20 plot, following so soon after the successful Allied D-day invasion of German-held France on June 6, 1944, added to his rage. British and American forces had pushed beyond the Normandy beaches along a fifty-mile front, recapturing territory that had been occupied by the Nazis since the 1940 blitzkrieg, the six-week lightning strike by the German army across France. Albert Speer, Hitler's minister for munitions and war production, said that after D-day, "All the military leaders whom I knew said at the time that the war was bound to end in October or November, since the invasion had been successful."[3]

Hitler ignored the naysayers, ordered the German army to continue fighting, and on December 16, 1944, he launched an attack like a staggered boxer's counterpunch that caught the Allies by surprise. General Dwight Eisenhower, supreme Allied commander in Europe, told his troops during the German thrust, later named the Battle of the Bulge, that the enemy "is fighting savagely to take back all you have won and is using every treacherous trick to deceive and kill you."[4] Eisenhower, elevated to a five-star general by President Franklin D. Roosevelt as the battle unfolded, wanted to take advantage, urging his men: "The enemy may give us the chance to turn his great gamble into his worst defeat." Despite the general's best efforts, Hitler inflicted the worst wartime atrocity on American troops in Europe.

At seven minutes before midnight on Monday, July 31, 1944, Adolf Hitler began an hourlong meeting with General Alfred Jodl, the fifty-four-year-old chief of operations of the German High Command, in a heavily fortified bunker in the Wolf's Lair.[5] Security had been increased after the assassination attempt eleven days earlier at Hitler's hideaway in the East Prussian forest, a rustic compound dominated by trees, camouflage netting, and concrete bunkers, but Jodl, an early Hitler supporter, remained in good standing. He had spent almost the entire war in a private bunker at Wolf's Lair, had been injured in the July 20 explosion, and would be tried by the victorious Allied forces at Nuremberg and executed in 1946 for crimes against humanity. Hitler relied on Jodl to translate his ideas into military orders and, unlike other fawning acolytes, the general had always spoken to his commander in chief with square-jawed confidence. However, on this day, he listened quietly as the Nazi leader proposed a counterattack.

Hitler, fifty-five years old, stooped like an octogenarian, and suffering the tremors of Parkinson's disease, delivered a rambling tirade against his July 20 enemies:[6] "Certainly there has been ongoing treason, and it's partly our fault. . . . We always acted too late against the traitors, out of consideration for the so-called army . . . although we already knew for a long time . . . that they were traitors. . . . We have to repel and drive away those low creatures—the lowest creatures in history ever to wear the soldier's uniform." Hitler then instructed Jodl to develop "a certain plan of ours—but that plan must not be distributed to the army groups. . . . You can't keep such thoughts from being immediately transmitted to the enemy these days, considering the lack of security within the inner army services." The Nazi leader left the details to Jodl but made clear he wanted a bold strike, a "battle brought to us by destiny—a battle of destiny that somehow cannot be avoided . . . but that it is really a kind of Hun battle in which you either stand, or fall and die." He was prepared to gamble: "I can't tell now where the last dice will fall but to use them where we can possibly create a change."

Hitler's secret instructions to Jodl on July 31, 1944, to plan a counterattack to turn the tide of the war, ignored earlier advice from his most competent generals. Field Marshal Gerd von

Rundstedt, a short man with a Hitler-like mustache, was sixty-nine years old in 1944—a military antique but with warrior blood. He became a career soldier like his father, who served in the Franco-Prussian War of 1870. Rundstedt was a staff officer during World War I, led the 1940 blitzkrieg in France, and was commander in chief in the West on D-day. He understood the power of logistics as well as military tactics and knew that after the successful Normandy landings, the endless parade of U.S. and British tanks and troops spelled disaster for Germany. At the end of June, he traveled to Berchtesgaden, Hitler's retreat in the Bavarian Alps near the Austrian border, to outline his concerns, but failed to impress the Nazi leader.[7] Rundstedt returned to his headquarters in France, telephoned his boss, Wilhelm Keitel, chief of the Armed Forces High Command, and told him they "better find a younger man to continue the battle." Keitel, a close confidante of Hitler's, asked what he thought they should do about the military situation, and Rundstedt shouted into the phone: "End the war, you fools!"

Hitler rewarded Rundstedt's honesty by firing him on Monday, July 3, 1944, and replacing him with Field Marshal Gunther von Kluge, a veteran of the early German victories in Poland, Russia, and France. Only seven years younger than Rundstedt, who was his commanding officer in 1940, but taller and more optimistic (at least initially), Kluge wore the same military medals on his chest. Little surprise that soon after arriving at his new headquarters, he came to the same conclusion, but the July 20 assassination attempt interrupted, giving him pause. Kluge had known about the conspiracy and had not reported it, making him vulnerable, but, days later, he sent a note to Hitler echoing Rundstedt's assessment:[8] "I arrived here with the firm intention of carrying out your orders to hold fast at all costs. But when one realizes that the price which must be paid consists of the slow but steady annihilation of our troops . . . then one cannot help entertaining the gravest doubts as to what the immediate future holds in store."

Kluge had taken a step toward the grave.

Less than a month later, Kluge disappeared during a trip to the front lines, and Hitler, who had suspected his loyalty after the defeatist letter, thought he might have secretly contacted the British to negotiate an armistice. Kluge turned up at his headquarters after a few hours, explaining that enemy aircraft had strafed his jeep, and was greeted with a message that Hitler had fired him as commander in chief in the West and summoned him back to Germany. Kluge understood what that meant and, on the drive back to Berlin on August 18, took poison to end his life, but not before penning a fawning farewell to Hitler:[9] "The German people have borne such untold suffering that the time has come to put an end to these horrors . . . My Fuhrer, I have always admired your greatness and military bearing in this gigantic struggle. . . . You have fought a great and honorable fight. Prove yourself now to be so great as to put an end . . . to this hopeless struggle. I take leave of you now, my Fuhrer, as one who . . . [has] done his duty to the last."

Hitler dismissed Kluge's deathbed flattery, telling Keitel, "It's not yet time for a political decision. I think I have proven enough in my life that I am able to gain political successes. I don't have to explain to anybody that I wouldn't let an opportunity . . . pass by. But it is, of course, childish and naïve to hope for a convenient political moment to do anything during this time of military defeat. Such moments can arise if we have successes."[10] Hitler expected Jodl's planned counterattack to deliver a victory, adding, we "continue the fight until the opportunity for a reasonable peace arises—one that is acceptable to Germany and can secure the life of later generations."

An acceptable peace to Hitler differed considerably from the interests of the German people, but the failed July 20 plot left no one to fight for the lives of ordinary men and women. Hitler gambled for personal glory while soldiers and citizens bore the costs, and this dichotomy, as with so many dictators, perverted his obligations to the country. He ignored the potential damage of his reckless venture and took egomania to a new level: "If the German people lose the war," he said, "it [*sic*] will have proved itself not worthy of me."[11]

H itler met in his Wolf's Lair bunker with a small group of trusted military advisers on Saturday, September 16, 1944, and swore them all to secrecy.[12] Jodl and Keitel attended, of course, and so did General Heinz Guderian, an early proponent of combining infantry and mechanized armor in a unit called a panzer division. Air force general Werner Kreipe represented Hermann Göring, head of the Luftwaffe, who was not invited, perhaps because the diminished performance of his aircraft versus the Allies had displeased Hitler. The Nazi leader would have been more displeased to know that Kreipe was a compulsive diarist, violating Hitler's strict ban on records of meetings other than official transcripts doctored to his pleasure. The general's uncensored notes offer an insider's preview of the Battle of the Bulge.

Jodl began the meeting by reviewing the western front—an unpleasant topic, since the Allies had liberated Paris a few weeks earlier and pushed the German army too close for comfort to the Rhine River. He lowered his voice to muffle his estimate of British and American superior troop strength compared with that of the German army, hoping that Hitler's impaired hearing, worsened by the July 20 explosion, missed the bad news. But when Jodl whispered the words "scarcity of heavy weapons, ammunition, and tanks," Hitler interrupted him with a dismissive wave and, after a moment of awkward silence, said: "I have just made a momentous decision." He then added dramatic flair by stabbing his finger at the map on the table in front of them, saying, "I shall go over to the counterattack—here out of the Ardennes, with the objective Antwerp."[13]

The carefully orchestrated announcement surprised everyone, except for Jodl, who had been working on the plan since meeting with Hitler at the end of July. The general remained as silent as stage scenery while Hitler explained targeting the Belgian city of Antwerp, a distant trophy deep in enemy territory, because it was the key port used by the Allied armies. He also said, more cryptically, that he wanted to "bust the seam between the British and American armies," and then, nodding in Kreipe's direction, added an operational detail: "The offensive should be launched during the bad weather period; then the enemy cannot fly either."[14]

Hitler's grand design followed a script from Germany's past. The planned counterattack recalled the spring offensive of World War I, a desperate thrust beginning March 21, 1918, by General Erich von Ludendorff, chief of staff to Field Marshal Paul von Hindenburg, to crush the British and French armies before massive American troop reinforcements arrived. The United States had entered the Great War in April 1917 but had been unprepared, taking almost a year before sending combat soldiers. Ludendorff knew that a fully committed America would prevail by outgunning Germany. Hitler, only a corporal during the first World War, had glorified his participation in the Ludendorff offensive: "It was my luck to be in the first two and the last of-fensive of 1918. They made on me the most tremendous impres-sions of my whole life; tremendous because for the last time, the struggle lost its defensive character and became as offensive . . . as it was [earlier] in 1914. In the German army trenches . . . men breathed anew, when after three years of hell, the day for squar-ing accounts had arrived."[15]

Ludendorff's wager failed and led to the German surrender on November 11, 1918, but Hitler had at least two reasons to expect better results. He thought that Britain and the United States formed a fragile partnership and might splinter with an attack aimed between the two armies: "What we have as oppo-nents are the greatest extremes that can be imagined . . . on one side a dying world empire, Britain, and on the other side a col-ony seeking an inheritance, the USA. . . . If a few heavy strikes were to succeed here, this artificially maintained united front could collapse at any moment with a huge clap of thunder."[16] Hitler misunderstood his adversaries and, worse, did not know it. He learned about America from watching Hollywood films, especially Laurel and Hardy slapstick comedies, but he should have looked in the mirror to see the hated image nurturing the marriage between U.S. president Franklin Roosevelt and British prime minister Winston Churchill. Hitler also heard about com-petition between American General George Patton, a pugnacious bulldog, and Britain's Field Marshal Bernard Montgomery, an egotistical peacock, which made entertaining drama on the silver screen but disappeared on the battlefield under General Dwight Eisenhower's touch.

Hitler also expected to succeed, unlike Ludendorff, because he would attack through the Ardennes Forest, and that made more sense. Rivers, streams, steep valleys, and dense woods crisscross the Ardennes like a spider's web, trapping unsuspecting tanks and artillery of a modern army. Most military strategists thought the rugged terrain, spread across France, Belgium, Luxembourg, and Germany, was impenetrable. France paid the price for that assessment in 1940, leaving the area lightly defended and allowing Germany to slice through the forest and conquer the country in six weeks. General Gerd von Rundstedt commanded the 1940 blitzkrieg across France, so it made considerable sense when Hitler announced at his "momentous decision" meeting on September 16 that he recalled Rundstedt to lead the counterattack.[17]

The old general would surprise his enemies again.

Headlines throughout the world during November 1944 hailed the Allies' march to the brink of the Rhine, threatening to trample the Third Reich and raising the stakes for Hitler's final bet. The *New York Times* led with the banner "To the Rhine," the *Irish Times* put "Americans Advance on Rhine 'Gateways,'" on its front page, but the *Manchester Guardian,* which did not mention Germany's most famous river, irritated Hitler most of all with the headline "Two Novembers."[18] The British newspaper compared Germany's current military position with November 1918, when the country surrendered, ending the Great War: "The Kaiser's armies were still able to carry out large scale offensive operations. . . . Today the German war machine is almost worn out. It is no longer working full blast. The cogs no longer fit together. . . . The situation for the Germans on Armistice Day, 1918, was, beyond comparison, more favorable than now."[19] The disrespect only hardened Hitler's determination to counterattack; to turn the Third Reich's heartbeat into a drum roll.

Chief of Staff Jodl had met with a handful of senior officers on Friday, November 3, to outline the Ardennes offensive, swearing them to secrecy by Hitler's order. General Hasso von Manteuffel, short in stature but with a big reputation, heavily decorated for bravery during battles in North Africa and Russia, and promoted by Hitler to lead the Fifth Panzer Army, recalled the formal oath he signed at the beginning of the meeting: "I had assumed that the conference would be merely routine . . . but a glance at the document . . . quickly showed this was to be an unusual meeting. . . . Each officer present had to pledge himself to complete silence . . . [and] should any officer break this pledge . . . his offense would be punishable by death." Manteuffel signed the document, thinking, "I had frequently attended top-secret conferences presided over by Hitler at Berchtesgaden or the Wolf's Lair, both before and after July 20, 1944, and this was the first time that I had seen a document such as [this] one."[20]

During the meeting, Jodl set Saturday, November 25, as the date for the counterattack, and asked Manteuffel to comment. The diminutive general said he would "do his utmost" to implement the plan, despite reservations about its wisdom, and recalls the horrified look on Jodl's face "when I went on to say that I did not see how the attack could possibly be launched successfully before December 15."[21] Jodl said, "Hitler would never agree to that," but Manteuffel stood his ground. He was right about the timing, and Hitler later accepted the delay, eventually agreeing to Saturday, December 16, as Null Tag, Germany's D-day.[22]

Manteuffel had a lengthy private conversation with Hitler after a briefing on Saturday, December 2, and the Nazi leader explained that a successful counterattack would be a public relations coup, buoying German morale and gaining renewed respect in the Allied countries. He then added a thought that raised goosebumps on Manteuffel's neck, shrinking the general to even less than his five-foot-four-inch frame: "I am determined to carry out the operation regardless of risks; even if the impending Allied attacks . . . should result in great loss of territory and of fortified positions. I am nevertheless determined to go ahead with this attack."[23] According to Manteuffel, Hitler added that it was time "to put everything on one throw of the dice."

Hitler's obsession with secrecy paid off. Not only did he threaten death to anyone leaking information, but he named the plan Watch on the Rhine, suggesting defense rather than offense, a subtle deception worthy of Her Majesty's Secret Service. Jodl contributed by calling his operational details Autumn Fog, a seasonal observation reflecting the need for unfavorable weather to ground Allied aircraft to help the attack succeed. When the Germans launched the Ardennes offensive at five thirty on Saturday morning, December 16, 1944, most Allied commanders were otherwise occupied, perhaps because they had been reading the favorable headlines. Christmas plans dominated for Britain's Field Marshal Montgomery, who had sent a letter by courier the day before to Eisenhower asking permission to return to England to spend the holiday with his son.[24] He also reminded Ike, as the general was called, of a £5 bet they had made a year earlier that the war would end before Christmas 1944. Montgomery had taken "the over" and Eisenhower "the under," so Montgomery asked for his money, writing, "For payment, I think, at Christmas." Eisenhower said that Monty would get the cash in his "Christmas stocking but not until Christmas Day." Ike still had nine days, and anything could happen, but that was before reports of the German offensive reached his headquarters, securing Montgomery's bet.

Gerd von Rundstedt's order of the day, intercepted by the Allies at eleven in the morning on December 16, should have sounded the alarm: "Soldiers of the Western front! Your great hour has come. Strong attacking armies have banded today against the Anglo-Americans. I don't have to add anything to this. You sense it all! We gamble everything! Carry with you the holy duty to give everything and to do superhuman efforts. For our fatherland and the Fuhrer."[25] Rundstedt made Hitler's giant wager sound like a crusade but failed to convince Eisenhower to skip the wedding of his orderly, Sergeant Mickey McKeogh, to Pearlie Hargrave, at the Trianon Palace Hotel in Versailles.[26] Later in the day, after reports of multiple penetrations of the Allied front lines, Ike finally alerted his staff: "This [is] no local attack," adding: "It was not logical for the enemy to attempt merely a minor offensive in the Ardennes."[27] Eisenhower understood the danger: "It was through this same region that the Germans launched their great attack of 1940 . . . led by the same commander we are now facing, von Rundstedt. It was possible that he hoped to repeat his successes of more than four years earlier."

The Germans advanced in the first few days, aided by thick fog and low clouds sheltering their tanks from American and British aircraft. They penetrated fifty miles into the center of Allied territory, creating a bulge in the battle line on the map—hence the encounter's name. But the Germans never came close to capturing the brass ring: the Belgian port of Antwerp. According to General Manteuffel, by Christmas Eve, the Allies had lanced the boil: "It was clear that the high-water mark of our operation had been reached. We now knew that we would never reach our objective."[28] He explained: "Perhaps the most decisive factor of all was the change in the weather. From December

23 and 24 . . . Allied Air Forces were able to operate freely: they found worthwhile targets throughout the whole area of our offensive. . . . The mobility of our forces decreased steadily . . . snow fell, and the temperature dropped, the scanty mountain roads were sheets of ice and movement by daylight became . . . impossible."

The Ardennes Forest caught the German army in its web of narrow passageways and slippery terrain, restoring its impenetrable reputation. Hitler refused to capitulate, so the battle raged until the end of January 1945, becoming one of the bloodiest of the war.[29] During the fighting, Henry Stimson, the American secretary of war (renamed secretary of defense in 1947), acknowledged that the enemy had cost the United States "severe" casualties, but, he added, "the German throw of the dice will have disastrous consequences for him."[30] Stimson was right on both counts. Tales of deception, brutality, and sorrow peppered the Battle of the Bulge to the end, but the greatest depravity came on day two, Sunday, December 17, near the small Belgian town of Malmédy. It gave new meaning to collateral damage from a desperate gamble.

H itler knew that the success of his surprise attack depended on speed and commitment, so he designated the newly created Sixth Panzer Army, consisting of Waffen SS battle groups, to spearhead the advance. Unlike the regular German army, the Wehrmacht, members of the Waffen SS belonged to the military branch of the SS, the Schutzstaffel, headed by Heinrich Himmler, who also ran the Gestapo, the sadistic police force. Members of the Waffen SS, like their Gestapo brethren, belonged to the Nazi Party, pledging their lives to Hitler like disciples in a cult. After the July 20 plot, Hitler trusted these fanatics far more than the professional soldiers, although he needed both, so he armed the Waffen SS battalions with the most advanced weapons. Lieutenant Colonel Joachim Peiper, a member of Hitler Youth as a teenager, a former administrative assistant to Himmler, and a veteran officer in the Waffen SS, benefited from Hitler's paranoia. The twenty-nine-year-old Peiper, a slim six-footer, led a force of more than a hundred tanks on December 16, including the newly manufactured King Tiger, a seventy-ton monster, plated with nearly impenetrable heavy armor.[31] His objective was the Meuse River, the first stop on the way to Antwerp.

On Sunday morning, December 17, Peiper's attack column encountered resistance from American soldiers near the tiny town of Malmédy, slowing his advance, but after a brief firefight, the outnumbered GIs surrendered. Peiper left his SS infantrymen in charge of the prisoners and led his tanks forward, determined to make up for lost time.[32] No one heard the lieutenant colonel give any instructions, but soon after he left, the SS troops herded more than a hundred American prisoners of war into a snow-covered field and opened fire with pistols and machine guns. Some of the POWs survived the massacre by hiding beneath their murdered comrades, but at least seventy-one American soldiers were killed in cold blood. Corporal Ted Paluch, a twenty-one-year-old GI, survived: "I was real lucky," he recalled years later, "as I was in the front end and only got hit slightly . . . and then anyone that moaned, they came around and they shot. I played dead and just lay there."[33] Paluch recognized they were SS by the distinctive skull, crossbones, and lightning insignia on their collars. He recalls laying stiff in the snow for about two hours, and escaping, along with several others, after "all the trucks and halftracks passed, and it was a little quiet."

News of the Malmédy massacre stunned American soldiers, first with disbelief and fear, and then anger a month later when GIs recaptured the area and discovered bodies buried beneath the snow. Some corpses remained frozen with their hands raised above their heads, still signaling surrender, while a medical orderly died with a bullet through his red cross armlet.[34] The small town of Malmédy had turned into a killing field in the Belgian countryside, synonymous with a war crime, which brought seventy-three men to trial in May 1946, a year after Germany surrendered.

The military trial in Dachau, the infamous Nazi concentration camp, featured Joachim Peiper and other members of his Waffen SS regiment as defendants.[35] Three surviving U.S. soldiers testified, with former lieutenant Virgil Lary of Lexington, Kentucky, making the most dramatic accusation:[36] "After the first of the machine gun fire, men fell dead and wounded all around me. The firing lasted about three minutes. . . . A man came by me, and I heard a pistol shot nearby, then I heard the sound of a new clip being inserted in a pistol." Lary paused, pointed a finger at one of the defendants, and said, "This is the man who fired two shots at an American prisoner of war." Private George Fleps blinked when Virgil Lary identified him as a murderer.[37]

Fleps was a lowly panzer soldier who thought he was following orders, which was no excuse, of course, but only a more senior officer could confirm wider responsibility. An affidavit submitted to the court by SS First Lieutenant Benoni Junker admitted that he ordered his tank commanders to "use terror methods in the treatment of war prisoners," and said that he was under orders not to take prisoners "if conditions warranted."[38] Four enlisted men said that, on the eve of the battle, they heard directly from Joachim Peiper to "drive recklessly, give no quarter, and take no prisoners."[39] But the most damning testimony came from Peiper himself, taking the stand in his own defense.

Peiper wore a drab military tunic without insignia, sat with his legs crossed, and was flanked by a female interpreter. He turned his sharp, narrow nose toward her while the prosecutor asked a question, and waited before answering, although he seemed to understand before she translated from English into German.[40] Peiper denied killing American POWs but admitted passing an order to lower commanders, which he had received from his superiors, to conduct the battle "stubbornly, with no regard for Allied prisoners of war, who will have to be shot if the situation makes it necessary and compels it."[41] Peiper did not shoot anyone at Malmédy. but those explicit orders made him as guilty as if he had pulled the trigger seventy-one times. Peiper's commanding officer, SS General Sepp Dietrich, added another link, saying that immediately before the battle began, "The Fuhrer said we would have to act with brutality and show no humane inhibitions."[42]

Soldiers like George Fleps had been trained to obey their superiors, but Hitler's ominous order of the day, signed two weeks earlier, increased the incentive: "This battle will decide whether the German people shall continue to exist or disappear. It demands complete devotion from each one of us: from the soldiers it demands . . . courage which defies death . . . from commanders it demands unyielding authority. These qualities will enable us to reestablish a desperate situation."[43] Soldiers thought that if the Ardennes offensive succeeded, no one would be punished, and if they failed, their sins would be buried with them. A young SS infantryman wrote to his sister in the predawn hours of December 16, 1944: "We attack to throw the enemy from our homeland. This is a holy task."[44] SS cavalry officer Philipp von Boeselager said of his men: "They almost took it for granted that they would die, but they were also brutal in their killing."[45]

In July 1946 the U.S. military court sentenced forty-three of the Malmédy defendants to death, including Peiper. Defense lawyers appealed, and in 1951 a second American military court cited technical errors and commuted the sentences; all of the defendants were released by Christmas 1956.[46]

Joachim Peiper had spent a total of twelve years in prison for the Malmédy massacre: about two months for each of the seventy-one documented murders. He then went to work training sales personnel for the Porsche and Volkswagen automobile companies.[47] In 1972 he moved to Traves, France, a sleepy village surrounded by farms, about eighty miles from the German border. Four years later, as the French celebrated Bastille Day, July 14, 1976, Peiper was shot dead and his house burned to the ground. A man representing a group called the Avengers telephoned a Paris newspaper the following day and claimed responsibility: "It is a warning to all Nazis hiding in France and Germany."[48]

H itler's desperate wager created a tailwind of destruction lasting more than thirty years. It could have been avoided. The Nazi leader told trusted aides before the attack, "We'll keep fighting this battle at all costs, until, like Frederick the Great said, one of our damned enemies gets tired, and until we get a peace that will secure life for the German nation for the next fifty or one hundred years."[49] Hitler's dream of a negotiated peace clashed with President Franklin Roosevelt's demand for unconditional surrender, a politically popular phrase in the United States, borrowed from Union general Ulysses S. Grant's decree early in the American Civil War. When Nazi propaganda minister Joseph Goebbels first heard those words in January 1943, he confided to a colleague, "I should never have been able to think up so rousing a slogan. . . . How can any German, whether he likes it or not, do anything but fight on with all his strength?"[50] Goebbels fueled Hitler's reckless counterattack in 1944, saying, "The Germans have nothing to lose and everything to gain."[51]

General Dwight Eisenhower, the Allied commander in Europe and future president of the United States, agreed with Goebbels. He sent a telegram in November 1944 to the Combined Chiefs of Staff in Washington, warning that the "enemy's continued stolid resistance" comes, in part, from "Nazi propaganda which is convincing every German that unconditional surrender means the complete devastation of Germany and her elimination as a nation."[52] Eisenhower understood that there are conditions to every surrender—as had Grant, agreeing at the end of the Civil War to allow soldiers of the surrendering Confederate army to keep their horses and sidearms.[53]

No one wanted to let Nazi war criminals such as Goebbels or Göring go unpunished, but Roosevelt could have altered Germany's incentives by showing a willingness to negotiate, at least publicly, changing the terms of engagement, and, perhaps, broadening Stauffenberg's conspiracy. Nothing is certain, but a negotiated peace in 1944 could have avoided Hitler's endgame and prevented the deadly consequences of his futile gamble, including the worst wartime atrocity inflicted on American troops in Europe.

PART IV

SOMETHING TO LOSE

CHAPTER 9

PRISON VIOLENCE

"When the judge said 'natural life,' it really was like getting the death sentence, because I knew I would die in prison," said Laura Bowers, an inmate at the Dwight Correctional Center, a Level One adult-female maximum security prison in Dwight, Illinois, about seventy miles southwest of Chicago.[1] Chief Judge Rodney Scott of the Macon County Circuit Court sentenced the twenty-two-year-old Bowers to life without parole for killing her husband, David Bowers, a state conservation police officer. Laura pleaded guilty in July 1990 to planning the murder with her lover, Ben McCreadie. They met while working as certified nurse's aides at an assisted-living facility and hatched the scheme so they could marry. McCreadie, also sentenced to life without parole, carried out the murder on Sunday, March 25, 1990, with the help of his roommate, by bludgeoning David Bowers with a lead pipe, strangling him with a hair blower cord, and slashing his throat with a knife.

Although Laura Bowers did not join in the actual assault, which occurred in Laura and David's apartment, she had secretly removed her husband's gun from the premises earlier in the day. Judge Scott said, "One cannot say she is not fully guilty."[2] An assistant state's attorney added, "When you look at the brutality, the cold-bloodedness, the calculated nature of this terribly brutal murder, then I believe no person would second-guess a sentence of life without parole."

Maximum sentencing guidelines have filled American prisons to overcapacity, and correction officers view long-term inmates, especially life-without-parole prisoners such as Laura Bowers and Ben McCreadie, like kegs of gunpowder. D'Antonio Washington, a thirty-one-year-old guard at the U.S. Penitentiary in Atlanta, died on Thursday, December 22, 1994, after being beaten with a hammer by an inmate. Kent B. Alexander, the United States attorney in Georgia who would prosecute the man accused of killing Officer Washington, said: "The increase in violence in the prisons is not one of America's great mysteries. There are more violent offenders in the system. They are serving longer sentences, and they feel they've got nothing to lose."[3]

Prisoners confirm the power of despair. A thousand inmates in the maximum security block of the California State Prison at Lancaster refused to come out of their cells for work, recreation, or meals to protest a new rule that would ban overnight family visits for inmates serving time for murder, spousal abuse, and sex crimes.[4] California began prison conjugal visits, one of only seven states with such a program, under tough-on-crime governor Ronald Reagan in 1968 as a way to lower homosexual rapes among convicts. Robert Parker, a forty-five-year-old inmate serving time for kidnaping and robbery, said that restricting the visits was all but certain to heighten tension inside the prison walls: "What incentive would a man have to do right?" Martha Riley, whose forty-eight-year-old husband is doing thirty-six years to life for murder, and who has had sex with her husband about every four months for the last eleven years, expanded on the same point: "What you're doing is creating a desperate subclass."

The California strike ended after four days, and a hearing was scheduled to examine the proposed ban on conjugal visits, but sex-related violence dominates prison life throughout the country. Randy Payne, a twenty-three-year-old felon serving a fifteen-year sentence for burglary and indecent exposure, wrote to his mother upon learning of his impending transfer to the maximum security Terrell Unit prison near Livingston, Texas, one of toughest and most deadly institutions in the state: "If you make it out of there without getting stabbed, you're lucky. If you make it out of there with all your teeth, you're one tough mother." A day after his arrival, Saturday, August 5, 1995, Payne's fear became a nightmare. According to subsequent reports, "Payne was confronted in a shower by a gang of convicts who demanded sex. When he refused, at least twenty convicts attacked him in a blood lust that stretched over two hours. Payne was pummeled with fists and with padlocks knotted inside socks, then kicked with steel-toed boots, in at least five locations in his cell block—all less than sixty feet from a guard. When the savagery ended, Payne was unconscious from severe head injuries. He died a week later at a Houston hospital."[5]

The 2001 report on male rape in U.S. prisons by the Human Rights Watch, an independent monitoring organization, cited Payne's murder as "one of the most tragic and violent cases" to come to its attention, but concludes that "overtly violent rapes are only the most visible and dramatic form of sexual abuse behind bars."[6] In most cases, "weak" prisoners become "the target of continuing sexual exploitation, both from the initial perpetrator and . . . from other inmates as well."[7] A Texas prisoner identified only as J.D. told investigators that after he was violently raped by his cell mate, "from that day on, I was classified as a homosexual and was sold from one inmate to the next."[8]

Convicts throughout the country confirmed the practice of "sexual slavery," although, the Human Rights Watch reports, "Texas has the worst record."[9] Andy Collins, who headed the agency that runs Texas's prisons, said the situation highlights a much broader and troubling trend: "We are seeing a larger group of tougher, more violent inmates who are predatory—and who we are going to have to keep isolated from themselves and others. They see themselves as invincible. They face long sentences for violent crimes. They have nothing to lose. They are and will continue to be a growing problem in growing numbers."[10]

Inmates facing life behind bars expect to die there, with little to gain from good behavior. Prison authorities like Collins and state prosecutors such as Georgia's Kent B. Alexander suggest that "lifers" are exceptionally violent as a result, and buttress that view with lurid tales that belong in a horror movie. However, the broader record contradicts their claim, despite the brutality of some lifers. Anecdotal evidence makes headlines, but the objective data discussed below show that life-without-parole inmates resemble members of the local chamber of commerce more than Murder Incorporated. Rewards for good conduct dominate for most lifers, a surprising result showing the power of incentives to neutralize misbehavior.

The prison population in the United States has increased almost fivefold since 1980, despite a decline in crime, and now stands as the highest incarceration rate in the world.[11] America imprisons 655 people per 100,000, compared with only 355 per 100,000 in Russia, suggesting that the United States resembles medieval Spain during the Spanish Inquisition more than does its old Cold War adversary. Drug-related sentences account for much of that growth, along with increased maximum-sentencing guidelines from the get-tough-on-crime wave of the 1990s. Prisoners serving life sentences in federal and state jails totaled more than 160,000 in 2016, or about 10 percent of the prison population. One-third of those inmates, 53,000, have no possibility of parole, making them potentially the most dangerous of all. Stories of lifer violence make front-page news, coloring the public's perception, and encouraging some to extrapolate the behavior of killers such as Richard Conner, Corey Fox, and the most notorious of all, Thomas Silverstein.

In 2009 thirty-eight-year-old Chicago native Richard Conner was serving a life sentence in the super-maximum-security Tamms Correctional Center, in Tamms, Illinois, home to the state's most dangerous criminals until it closed in 2013.[12] He had been convicted of murdering a jewelry store clerk during a burglary in 1991 that netted $200. Conner had entered the store, asked to buy a watch, pulled a handgun, and yelled at the clerk, "I'm going to kill you!"—which he did by shooting him in the chest. Originally housed in the Cook County Jail, Conner was sent to the super-max Tamms in August 2006 as punishment for assaulting a prison staffer. While at Tamms, he attempted suicide and was transferred to the maximum security Stateville Correctional Center near Joliet for treatment. He was placed in a cell, about the size of a large walk-in closet, with Jameson Leezer, a thirty-seven-year-old petty criminal nearing the end of a five-year sentence for car theft. Two weeks later, on Thursday, April 2, 2009, Conner emerged from his cell and announced, "I strangled my cell mate."

The murder should not have been a surprise, especially after the two inmates had asked to be separated and Conner had told a prison worker that he intended to kill his cell mate. Leezer's family sued and won an undisclosed settlement, Conner received a second life sentence, and Assistant State's Attorney Steve Platek said after the sentencing, "It just seems crazy that he was ever put in a cell with this guy."

The prison officials at Stateville failed to learn from the same fatal error made five years earlier at the Menard Correctional Center, located about three hundred miles south in the Illinois town of Chester. Menard housed a number of serial killers, including Andre Crawford, Milton Johnson, and the disreputable John Wayne Gacy, who had murdered thirty-three young men in the 1970s. By comparison, Corey Fox, a goateed thirty-four-year-old inmate at Menard, serving a life sentence for murder during a botched home burglary, resembled a misbehaving schoolboy.[13] He wanted privacy, a scarce commodity in jail, and told a prison social worker of "urges to kill and dismember my cell mate." Fox almost made good on his threat in 2002, pummeling his bunk mate until he succeeded in getting a single-cell accommodation.

Fox was reevaluated the following year and then paired with Joshua Daczewitz, a pudgy, bespectacled, younger prisoner serving a seven-year sentence for arson. Fox objected again to having a cell mate and said later that he had given a correction officer a note threatening to "erase" Daczewitz. On Saturday, February 28, 2004, two weeks before Joshua Daczewitz's scheduled release, Corey Fox choked him with a braided bedsheet and then strangled him to death with his hands.

Fox explained later: "Being housed in solitary confinement with another person, unable to escape that person's presence, habits, or tactics, is like wearing a corset made of nails and explosives."[14] Despite the imagery, Fox was sentenced to a second life term, and, in a subsequent lawsuit, the court approved a $150,000 settlement payment from the state of Illinois to the Daczewitz family but dismissed charges of neglect against the Illinois Department of Corrections and the Menard Correctional Center. The warden of Menard at the time, Eugene McAdory Jr., admitted poor judgment: "Sixty percent of the inmates at Menard ain't never getting out. It was the wrong place for Daczewitz to be housed."[15] McAdory was fired several months after the murder, perhaps for assaulting the English language, but his double negatives suggest that lifers should be segregated to protect the rest of the prison population.

The poster child for lifer violence is Thomas Silverstein, placed in solitary confinement in 1983 at age thirty-one and remaining there until his death in 2019, when he looked like a mustachioed grandfather but was considered the most dangerous prisoner in America.[16] Silverstein grew up in Long Beach, California, in a middle-class neighborhood where he was bullied by other kids who mistakenly thought he was Jewish. His criminal history began with a routine armed robbery in 1971, sending him to California's San Quentin State Prison for four years. He was then paroled and rearrested in 1977 for repeating the same crime. His next stop was the US penitentiary in Leavenworth, Kansas, where he joined with members of the Aryan Brotherhood in the prison drug trade and murdered a fellow inmate who had refused to help smuggle heroin into the jail. Silverstein was sentenced to life without parole and transferred in 1980 to the U.S. penitentiary at Marion, Illinois, a maximum security prison labeled the New Alcatraz. It was the perfect place for more murder.

The Marion penitentiary opened in 1963 to replace the famous Rock, as Alcatraz was known, after the island prison in San Francisco Bay closed and became a tourist attraction operated by the National Park Service. Marion soon housed more dangerous criminals than its infamous predecessor. According to the crew-cut warden, Harold Miller, who was at Marion when Silverstein arrived, and who had begun his career as a guard at Alcatraz: "Judges sentence criminals to prison to protect society. Wardens send prisoners to Marion . . . to protect other prisoners."[17] A forty-five-year-old inmate sporting a green bandana confirmed, "Most men in here have no hope of getting out. . . . People are on edge. There's a lot of paranoia. . . . Society has created a monster with this place."[18]

Racial turmoil infested prison life in the 1960s and 1970s, reflecting broader American society, and reached a boiling point in Marion soon after Silverstein arrived. Gang warfare, pitting the white supremacist Aryan Brotherhood against an African American gang called the D.C. Blacks, exploded on Sunday, November 22, 1981, when Silverstein allegedly strangled D.C. Blacks member Robert M. Chappelle.[19] Although Silverstein denied the crime, Chappelle's friend, Raymond "Cadillac" Smith, planned to avenge the murder but was killed before he got the chance. Silverstein and another inmate stabbed Cadillac, a leader of the D.C. Blacks, sixty-seven times while he showered on Monday, September 27, 1982, and then displayed their handiwork—perhaps to deter to future assailants—by parading his body up and down the narrow catwalks. Silverstein was placed in solitary confinement, shackled in chains whenever transported out of his cell, and put under constant guard. He still managed a final act of brutality that crowned him America's Worst Prisoner.

At ten o'clock on the morning of October 22, 1983, Silverstein shuffled in chains along the catwalk, returning to his cell from the shower, escorted by three guards.[20] He paused in front of another cell, faced a fellow inmate ostensibly to talk, and then turned around holding an eighteen-inch knife fashioned from a bed frame. Silverstein then pinned correction officer Merle Clutts, a fifty-one-year-old grandfather scheduled to retire in less than a year, against the wall and stabbed him forty times before the other guards could subdue him. Silverstein received another life sentence for the murder, but in his defense, he claimed that Clutts had tormented him by, among other things, smudging the paintings he had created as part of his artwork hobby.

Norman Carlson, director of the Federal Bureau of Prisons, explained Clutts's death and other murders at Marion with a familiar refrain: "These inmates were already serving life sentences in the disciplinary section of the most maximum security prison in the country. They knew there was nothing else the federal prison system could do to them. They knew they had nothing to lose."[21]

Scrapbook snapshots of lifers Thomas Silverstein, Corey Fox, and Robert Conner portray violence, but they surface because grisly stories sell newspapers, not because they reflect broader prison reality. A richer portrait emerges upon further investigation. Twenty-year-old James Paluch Jr. received a sentence of life without parole in October 1991 for the unprovoked sniper killing on a Philadelphia street corner of a fifty-nine-year-old woman who was waiting for a bus to take her home from work. Paluch did not know her.[22] He pointed a rifle from his third-floor apartment window and pulled the trigger, shooting her through the heart.

Paluch has served time in five different Pennsylvania prisons and claims that inmates jailed for life usually make model prisoners: "Although you will rarely hear a lifer call a prison home, we collectively understand that due to the length of our sentences, this institution is literally Home. When things go wrong . . . it is the lifers who speak up. . . . To put it simply, lifers are the stabilizing force for prison management."[23] A past president of the

Pennsylvania Lifer's Association at the State Correctional Institution at Huntingdon, he added, "I would certainly not argue that every lifer in Pennsylvania is a model inmate, but a large majority of us are indeed examples that other inmates would do well to follow."

Paluch's point may be self-serving, but a number of correction officers support his story. Lieutenant Michael McDonald, an official at the California super-maximum-security Pelican Bay State Prison in Crescent City, said that unlike short-termers serving less than a decade, life-without-parole inmates generally stay out of trouble: "When you have the light at the end of the tunnel, you get cocky sometimes," he observed. "Your life prisoners are a little more serious about doing time. After a few years, this place starts to look more and more like home."[24] Wayne Estelle, who oversaw 1,100 inmates as warden of the California Men's Colony at San Louis Obispo, said that lifers "recognize they are going to be here for a while, and they want to live in a fairly comfortable atmosphere."[25]

California's balmy weather is not the explanation. Bill Slack, whose fatherly presence made him the best desk lieutenant at Kansas's Leavenworth penitentiary, understood why imprisoned murderers might avoid conflict: "The bottom line is that we come in here every day, do our job, and go home. These inmates are here twenty-four hours a day, and this is their home and their world."[26] Tom Page, warden at Illinois's Menard Correctional Center, where lifer Corey Fox murdered his cell mate, favors long-termers who have already adjusted: "As they mature," he explained, "it finally sinks into them that they will be here a long time, and they better make the best of it."[27]

Menard has an active lifer association, with eighty-five members gathering once a month at meetings that resemble Alcoholics

Anonymous, where they discuss depression, isolation, and hope-lessness. They also sponsor programs to give meaning to their lives, such as selling snacks and clothing within the prison to support a nearby youth center. Joe Coleman, a fifty-six-year-old past president of Menard Lifers, added: "You can't get away from the fact that you wake up in prison and you go to sleep in prison, day after day. It's reality. You have to accept that. But through the group, we try to instill self-worth and self-confidence. We want to show the youngsters coming in that no matter how dismal life looks, there is always hope."[28]

Lifers can hope to improve their lot. The most violent sit in solitary confinement, like Thomas Silverstein at Marion, endur-ing the pain of isolation, while others join activities reserved for the well behaved, like inmates at the Louisiana State Penitentiary at Angola performing in a rodeo show. Burl Cain, the warden from 1995 to 2016 of the largest maximum security prison in Louisiana, where 90 percent of inmates will remain until they die, introduced the show for prisoners to demonstrate their skills. The press reported, "Many of these black sheep of society lead shadow lives as artists, newspaper editors, country singers, and, five times a year, stars of a prison rodeo and arts-and-crafts fair, where convicts who've earned the right get to buck broncs and straddle bulls, as well as mingle with sell-out crowds of happy visitors."[29] Lane Nelson, a lifer at Angola, said, "The warden puts purposes out there for prisoners to attach themselves to, and that's what you need."

A convicted murderer identified only as Thomas, twenty years into a life-without-parole sentence at an unnamed East Coast penitentiary, gave a middle-class explanation for good be-havior: "When somebody gets a life sentence . . . they come here and they want to make life the best they can for themselves. They want honor visits. They want to be able to talk to their families on the phone whenever they want to. They want a nice cell with air conditioning, so they're going to abide by the rules and do the best they can."[30]

W hich profile of lifer behavior tells the truth: reckless violence or model citizen? Anecdotal evidence suffers from what experts call selection bias—a small sample designed to tell a tale, such as extrapolating New York Yankees pitcher Don Larsen's perfect game in the 1956 World Series to make him the best pitcher in baseball. Larsen's feat—the only postseason perfect performance in the sport's history—remains a Picasso, but he was an average hurler during his fourteen-year major league career, winning eighty-one games and losing ninety-one. His signature victory over the Brooklyn Dodgers made him a legend but did not get him into the National Baseball Hall of Fame. For similar reasons, individual acts of lifer brutality or honor, although worthy of attention, are just small pieces of an elaborate mosaic. The data on prison infractions from large samples of inmate behavior paint a fuller picture.

A study of the misconduct records of more than 9,000 inmates in the Florida Department of Corrections, published in the journal *Criminal Justice and Behavior*, benefits from big data.[31] The sample includes 1,897 inmates sentenced to life without parole and 7,147 serving terms between ten and thirty years, permitting formal tests of whether lifers misbehaved more often than shorter-term inmates. The analysis shows that "inmates serving terms of less than twenty years were most often involved in prison violence," while "life-without-parole inmates were similar to other long-term inmates held at the same custody level."[32]

An earlier study, published in the *Journal of Criminal Justice,* conducted interviews with more than fifty-nine prisoners and concluded that "short-term prisoners . . . treat any exchange between inmate and officer as a confrontation [while] . . . long-term inmates have learned to circumvent potentially 'sensitive' situations."[33] Interviews with officers at the Utah State Prison, published in the *Prison Journal,* make a similar observation: "[Lifers] cope probably better. . . . They learn how to work the system. They have the best jobs, and they know how to get what they want. The longer they are here, the better they cope with the system."[34] During a meeting with fellow long-termers discussing rising tension within prison, Pennsylvania inmate James Paluch Jr. urged his lifer buddies to help maintain the peace: "You got all these young guys coming in here. They don't care about nobody but themselves. . . . We have to step up, talk to these young bucks, and teach them the same way we were taught."[35]

At California's Correctional Training Facility in Soledad, lifers have taken Paluch's plea one step further. Kennaray Harris, twenty-four years into a life sentence, founded a prison program called Life-C.Y.C.L.E. (Careless Youth Corrected by Lifers' Experience).[36] He and his fellow inmates serving life sentences run activities to help short-timers at Soledad prepare for when they are released. Kennaray explained the success so far, which had about a hundred participants who met weekly for twenty-five weeks: "Nothing is new to us. Someone in this room has done it before. Our goal is to change the way these soon-to-be-released men view the world and their place in it. We want to make sure they find their niche."

Having nothing to lose promotes reckless behavior in prison just like everywhere else, but that attitude leads short-term inmates to cause the most trouble. Their short horizons soften punishments, so they misbehave, while penalties linger for lifers, keeping them in line. Prison authorities incentivize good behavior further by awarding privileges that give long-term inmates something to lose if they become violent.

Well-behaved lifers in maximum security facilities often become trustee prisoners with little oversight. In Louisiana, for example, a dozen inmates serving life sentences work as waiters, butlers, cooks, and other staff members at the governor's mansion in Baton Rouge.[37] At Angola, under warden Burl Cain's direction, prisoners built a nine-hole golf course on the premises for public use, and trustees keep the fairways playable by mowing the grass. Forty-eight-year-old Frederick Griffin, a trustee serving a life sentence for second-degree murder, gets up at four thirty in the morning to ride the mower, smell the fresh-cut grass, and watch the players. Golf was never his game: "It was always too slow for me," he said. "I liked basketball." But Griffin keeps the job: "It makes me feel like I'm free."[38]

Forty-seven-year-old lifer Richard Mikkelson, who, like Griffin, became a trustee with good behavior, was on the work crew that built the course, called Prison View because of the skyline. He is proud: "I don't know how they build these things out there on the streets. But we did it with shovels and rakes and hoes."[39] Mikkelson learned something about the game during the construction. "The par depends on the hazards and the length of the fairway." But the real lesson came from watching the players. "A golf course is a place to meet people," Mikkelson said, adding that if he ever got out of Angola, he would know where to network: "The main two places you go is a golf course and church."

Lifers may not like to call prison "home," but most behave that way. At last look, Ben McCreadie, who brutally murdered Officer David Bowers because he wanted to marry Mrs. Bowers, and received a sentence of life without parole, had been housed in Joliet Correctional Center for twelve years. When the maximum security wing at Joliet closed in 2002, McCreadie prepared for transfer by packing his bags along with the other inmates, but he reminisced like a displaced orphan:[40] "In a way, you're saying good-bye to a piece of you. You've done so much here. You have so many memories." McCreadie had become Joliet's in-house landscaper, planting lilies, petunias, and irises to flank the outdoor walkways. Thinned by years of prison food, and wearing a scraggly beard, he said: "I was known as the flower guy."

Not every lifer behaves like McCreadie, a newly sensitive man who clearly takes pride in his craft, but the data show that his profile fits prison misconduct records better than the likes of Thomas Silverstein. Many factors contribute to making hardened criminals into responsible jailhouse citizens, but having something to lose underlies it all. The next chapter examines whether that same strategy can curb suicide bombers.

CHAPTER 10

MOHAMED ATTA AND SUICIDE TERRORISTS

On Tuesday, August 25, 1987, Mario Tuti, a neo-Fascist Italian terrorist serving consecutive life terms for killing two policemen and conducting a bombing spree in the mid-1970s, led a revolt in the Porto Azzurro prison on the island of Elba, the famous exile home of Napoléon Bonaparte. He and five other inmates held twenty-two hostages in the jail's infirmary, including the prison director, two psychologists, a woman social worker, and eighteen guards. Armed with guns, knives, and explosives, the forty-year-old Tuti vowed to kill them all unless the authorities provided a bulletproof car and a helicopter for their escape. Mario had a violent history even in jail, murdering a fellow inmate a few years earlier who he considered "a traitor."[1] Tuti warned the police, "We will blow up all the hostages if you come in" and then called the Italian press to gain further credibility: "We're all lifers. We have nothing to lose."

Mario Tuti did not look like a terrorist. He wore large, black-rimmed glasses like a professor and had a thick black mustache like Groucho Marx. He had studied at the Faculty of Architecture in Florence and worked in the municipality of the town of

Empoli, but his indiscriminate bombings during 1974 to promote a Fascist revolution gave the authorities good reason to worry. More than two thousand Italian police surrounded the prison infirmary, including parachutists and fifty members of the Interior Ministry anti-terrorist squad known as the Leatherheads. Pope John Paul II told an audience of six thousand pilgrims, "I pray to the Lord that He may touch the heart of those who have in their hands the fate of so many people."

The mayor of Porto Azzurro, Maurizio Papi, who was also the prison doctor, knew the inmates and believed they would execute the hostages. He urged the police to grant the prisoners' request for a helicopter "to bring the revolt to a peaceful conclusion." Papi need not have worried. On September 2, eight days after the siege began, the six convicted murderers ended their revolt through a representative of Amnesty International. Relatives of the hostages waiting outside the prison cried with joy, and the town's church bells rang in celebration.

The leader of the uprising, Mario Tuti, had threatened to kill everyone but now asked for understanding: "We did not use violence . . . but we had no hope but to try to escape." Although Tuti was a murderer and a convicted terrorist, he was not a suicide bomber. He and his fellow inmates wanted to live, so they surrendered. Suicide terrorists do not behave that way. They expect to die along with their targets, which is how nineteen members of the militant Islamist group Al Qaeda succeeded in killing nearly three thousand people on Tuesday, September 11, 2001.

Suicide bombers terrify because they are so effective. The 9/11 disaster killed more people than any other foreign attack on U.S. soil, eclipsing the previous record of 2,403 in the

Japanese bombing of Pearl Harbor on Sunday, December 7, 1941. Both attacks changed America forever. Pearl Harbor brought the United States into World War II, a battle against Fascism, and 9/11 launched the war on terror, a battle against fanaticism. But there is an important difference. World War II ended with the defeat of Germany and Japan, but the war against terror continues because suicide bombers have no "return address." Terrorists cannot be defeated on the battlefield because they hide among civilians when not active. They also spread fear and carnage randomly, which is how they force us to disrupt our daily lives with unprecedented precautions.

Air travelers now endure security checks once reserved for visitors to Fort Knox, and tolerate personal searches resembling a medical check-up. In 2002 Congress established the U.S. Department of Homeland Security to oversee all domestic emergencies, especially terrorist threats, and the agency has enlisted local police departments by disbursing funds to enhance public safety. Police officers now have high-powered weapons with night-vision capability, biohazard suits, and advanced communications devices once used only by elite combat units such as the Navy SEALs. All of this in the name of heightened security against a terrorist threat that Americans once thought belonged exclusively to Europe, Africa, and Asia. September 11, 2001, changed that thinking.

Some worry that making local police resemble a Special Forces platoon is overkill, more harmful than helpful, but that ignores evidence that America became deadlier after 9/11. In the eighteen years following 9/11, mass shootings in the United States (defined as a lone gunman killing at least four people in a public space) took 601 lives, more than double the 257 in the previous eighteen years.[2] Comparing the number of shootings during the two periods tells the same sordid tale. The high-profile massacre at Colorado's Columbine High School on April 20, 1999, in which two heavily armed students roamed the building, killing twelve of their schoolmates, one teacher, and wounding more than two dozen others, was one of thirty-two mass shootings in the years before 9/11; the most deadly of all, the Las Vegas Strip massacre of October 1, 2017, carried out by a lone gunman firing down from a thirty-second-floor casino hotel window, killing sixty people, was one of sixty-one after 9/11.[3] Homegrown gunmen in the United States may not always want to commit suicide, but the evidence suggests they resemble copycat killers emboldened by the events of September 11, 2001. Destroying the World Trade Center and attacking the Pentagon were not the first suicide bombings, but their notoriety incentivized mass shooters seeking the spotlight.

The car bombing of the U.S. Marine barracks in Beirut, Lebanon, on October 23, 1983, killing 241 service personnel, launched the modern era of suicide terrorists.[4] On that same day, a suicide bomber drove a truck into a Beirut building just two miles away and murdered 58 French paratroopers inside. The attacks were traced to Hezbollah, a terrorist organization based in Lebanon with ties to Iran and Syria, but neither government accepts responsibility for Hezbollah's actions, making it difficult to prevent future massacres by punishing those countries. A total of 315 documented suicide terrorist attacks occurred between 1980 and 2003, one of the deadliest periods in the history of suicide bombing, but nothing compared with the last year of World War II.

The Japanese military, desperate to stop America's advance in the Pacific during 1944, created a special unit of pilots called kamikazes: conscripts and volunteers who intentionally crashed their bomb-filled planes into U.S. ships, killing themselves in the process.[5] The kamikazes carried out nearly 3,850 suicide bombings and killed more than twelve thousand U.S. servicemen, a lethal record of effectiveness. The attacks ended when Japan surrendered on August 15, 1945, which makes the kamikaze episode less relevant to profiling today's suicide bombers. Kamikazes were not stateless terrorists but belonged to a standing army that stopped fighting when its country succumbed. Silencing the kamikazes in 1945 does not show how to deter suicide terrorists who disappear among civilians when threatened. Moreover, kamikazes hit only military targets, a legitimate wartime objective, while Al Qaeda suicide bombers destroyed the World Trade Center filled with noncombatants. Al Qaeda terrorists have more in common with the Assassins of the eleventh century than with the kamikazes of the twentieth.

The Assassins were a small Islamic sect based primarily in the mountains of northwestern Iran. Outnumbered and despised by their more moderate coreligionists, trained in close combat, especially in using a dagger, they began to murder Muslim leaders considered impious, preferably in public to spread terror. They expected a reward of eternity in Islamic paradise. Legend has it that the first successful Assassin killed the Great Sultan Malik Shah of Persia in 1092 and shouted immediately after the attack, "The killing of this devil is the beginning of bliss!"[6] He was then martyred by the Sultan's bodyguards. Bernard Lewis, professor of Near Eastern Studies at Princeton University, concluded, "The Assassins are the true predecessors of many of the Islamic terrorists of today."[7]

Lewis may be right, but religion cannot be the whole story of modern suicide bombers; secular terrorists accounted for almost 25 percent of bombings toward the end of the twentieth century.[8]

The behavioral approach detailed below dominates Islamic extremism in explaining today's suicide bomber, covering nonbelievers and the pious alike. The framework will also show that terrorists have something to lose, which is the secret to stopping them. Professor Lewis made Al Qaeda a good place to start.

A letter with final instructions found among the belongings of Mohamed Atta, the thirty-three-year-old pilot-hijacker of the first plane to hit the World Trade Center on 9/11, made clear his motivation. He was an architectural engineer with a mathematical brain but a fundamentalist heart, believing that eternal life in the hereafter dominated his brief stay on earth. The letter read: "Those who prefer the afterlife over this world should fight for the sake of God. . . . Do not suppose that those who are killed for the sake of God are dead; they are alive."[9] The final words in the document carried a message for his coconspirators: "Afterward, we will all meet in the highest heaven, God willing." Life on earth is a path to paradise, according to Atta, so he had everything to gain by sacrificing himself in a holy mission. The asymmetric payoff to a martyr's death turned the normally reserved Atta into a deadly missile.

Mohamed el-Amir Atta was not born to be a terrorist.[10] He was raised in a Cairo suburb in a modern Muslim family. His father, a successful lawyer, bought a vacation home on the Mediterranean coast, and his older sisters pursued careers in medicine and academia. A strict disciplinarian, his father worried that Mohamed was too shy as a child and blamed his wife for "raising him as a girl."[11] He complained that "she never stopped pampering him." Mohamed, a wiry five foot seven inches, was studious, respectful of authority, and not outwardly religious, although his cousin recalled that whenever belly dancers appeared on television, a popular Egyptian obsession, Mohamed would leave the room. Neighbors do not remember seeing the family in the local mosque. After graduating in 1990 from Cairo University, one of the most prominent schools in Egypt, Mohamed went to Germany to study urban planning. It transformed his life.

Atta arrived in Hamburg in the summer of 1992, found a local mosque, and began to attend regularly. He observed a strict Islamic diet—no pork or alcohol—and abstained from socializing at clubs and sporting events. He kept a copy of the Koran near his bed, prayed five time a day, and fasted on holidays. In 1996, after a pilgrimage to Mecca, Saudi Arabia, he joined the al-Quds mosque in Hamburg, where the outspoken and flamboyant Islamist Mohammad Haydar Zammar preached. Atta wrote a will dedicating his life and death to Allah and forbade women to visit his grave.[12] But his transformation had occurred much earlier, according to his German landlord. Soon after arriving in Hamburg, Atta had said: "I am abroad now, I am grown up. Now I can decide on my own."[13] Perhaps his overbearing father had planted a seed that suddenly flowered like a deadly water hemlock.

Ziad Jarrah, the Lebanese pilot-hijacker of United Airlines flight 93, which crashed in Somerset County, Pennsylvania, after a passenger revolt on September 11, 2001, wrote to his girlfriend, Aysel Sengun, the day before his suicide mission: "I did not escape from you, but I did what I was supposed to do, and you should be very proud of me."[14] He said that soon they would live in a place "where there are no problems, and no sorrow, in castles of gold and silver." Jarrah came from an even more prosperous family than Atta. His parents owned a condominium in Beirut, a vacation home in the countryside, drove a Mercedes, and sent Ziad to private schools. Aysel said later, "Whenever he or I needed money, I just had to call Ziad's parents . . . and they asked how much I needed [and] they would always send over two or three times as much."[15] Ziad was a poor student, more interested in girls than in classes, but he became radicalized like Mohamed Atta after moving to Hamburg. They both attended the local al-Quds mosque and committed to holy war despite their comfortable upbringings.

Atta and Jarrah trained in Afghanistan with Al Qaeda during 1999, learning basic military weaponry—everything from pistols and sniper rifles to dynamite and grenade launchers. Atta met with Osama bin Laden, Al Qaeda's Saudi Arabian founder, to choose their final targets for September 11, including the World Trade Center and the Pentagon.[16] But, like other suicide bombers, they had become religious zealots beforehand; recruits were not admitted to Al Qaeda training camps unless they were already devout.[17] Four months before the 9/11 attacks, Sheikh Ikrima Sabri, the Grand Mufti of Jerusalem, said: "As much as you love life—the Muslim loves death and martyrdom."[18] Paradise drove their mission.

Palestinian suicide bombers, well educated and middle class like Atta and Jarrah, who attacked civilian targets in Israel, gave the same motivation. An interview with a member of the terrorist organization Hamas, identified only by the initial S, described the attraction of ultimate sacrifice: "It's as if a very high, impenetrable wall separated you from paradise or hell. Allah has promised one or the other to his creatures. So, by pressing the detonator, you can immediately open the door to paradise—it is the shortest path to heaven."[19] When asked what would happen if the operation failed, S replied, "We made an oath on the Koran, in the presence of Allah—a pledge not to waver. . . . All martyrdom operations, if done for Allah's sake, hurt less than a gnat's bite." Another member of Hamas gave visual directions to paradise: "It's very, very near, right in front of our eyes. It lies beneath the thumb. On the other side of the detonator."

The lure of eternity in heaven trivializes the sacrifice, making the asymmetric payoff to a suicide mission infinitely attractive. According to one recruit: "The power of the spirit pulls us upward while the power of material things pulls us downward. Someone bent on martyrdom becomes immune to the material pull."[20] This skewed calculation of religious fundamentalists explains the excess of volunteers among Islamic terrorist organizations. Murad Tawalbi, a nineteen-year-old suicide bomber from the West Bank town of Jenin, who was arrested before carrying out his mission in Haifa, Israel, thanked his brother for recruiting him: "He wasn't trying to make me wear an explosive belt. He was giving me a ticket to heaven. Because he loves me, he wants me to become a martyr. Because martyrdom is the most exalted thing in our religion. Not just anyone gets the chance to be a martyr."[21]

The connection between religion and suicide bombing disappears with the Tamil Tigers, a secular organization in Sri Lanka that holds the record for the most suicide bombings toward the end of the twentieth century. This Marxist-Leninist group, dedicated to establishing an independent country for the Tamil people in Sri Lanka, accounted for 76 of the 315 documented suicide bombings between 1980 and 2003.[22] The Tamil Tigers assassinated Rajiv Gandhi, son of former prime minister Indira Gandhi, during the 1991 Indian election campaign because they feared he would win and favor peacekeeping policies with the Sri Lanka government.[23] Tamil Tigers have assassinated a Sri Lankan president, defense minister, and national security adviser, along with moderate Tamil politicians opposed to their violence. None of their missions relate to religion, but a close look at Tamil Tigers suicide bombers shows that many reap an asymmetric payoff, just like their Islamic counterparts, but for very different reasons.

The most famous Tamil suicide bomber, a woman known by the single name Dhanu, stood a few feet away from Rajiv Gandhi on Tuesday, May 21, 1991, stepped forward with a flower to greet the famous Indian politician, and detonated a bomb concealed in a body belt beneath her sari.[24] The explosion killed Gandhi, Dhanu, and more than a dozen others, including the Tamil Tigers photographer whose surviving film recorded the unfolding horror. Dhanu left no explanation for her act, but the *New York Times* reported that Indian soldiers in Sri Lanka had once killed two of her brothers and had raped her during the encounter.[25] Dhanu's decision seems like a personal vendetta, a blood feud not obviously applicable to other Tamil terrorists. Except for one strange coincidence: many suicide bombers in Sri Lanka are women with similar stories.

Female suicide bombers in the Muslim world arouse less suspicion than men because they are so scarce. In 2003 a commander in charge of recruiting future Islamic terrorists said: "The body has become our most potent weapon. When we searched for new ways to resist the security complications facing us, we discovered that our women could be an advantage."[26] But that is not true for Tamil Tigers, where women have taken an active role from the very beginning. Dhanu belonged to a specialized female suicide unit called Black Tigresses. Of the estimated ten thousand recruits in Sri Lanka during the 1990s, about four thousand were female, a surprisingly high proportion compared with Muslim terrorists; all 9/11 suicide bombers were male.[27]

Women recruits join the Tamil Tigers for a variety of reasons, just like men. Some are unemployed and seek a purpose; others are nationalists fighting for their homeland; and still others want to avenge a relative's murder. But many women volunteer because they have been raped and are outcasts in their local communities. They become suicide bombers because they are desperate.

According to author Kate Fillion, who traveled through Sri Lanka with the Tamil Tigers, "A raped woman can go from being a source of dishonor to her family to being a source of pride in a culture of martyrdom."[28] Fillion reports newspaper editorials admonishing Sri Lankan soldiers "to stop raping Tamil women at checkpoints because they were just creating more operatives." Ana Cutter, a former editor of Columbia University's *Journal of International Affairs,* reports that a Tamil woman said, "Acting as a human bomb is an understood and accepted offering for a woman who will never be a mother."[29] And investigative journalist Jan Goodwin, after visiting Sri Lanka, said, "Rape is something many female suicide bombers have in common. Considered spoiled goods and unmarriageable in their patriarchal cultures, they view becoming human bombs as a form of purification."[30] She tells the story of Menake, a "twenty-seven-year-old woman with long black hair, neatly pulled back from her chocolate-colored skin—the kind of person you'd trust with your kids," who became a suicide bomber after having been raped as a child by her father. On her mission to kill the Sri Lankan prime minister, Menake wore a sequined top to hide the explosive vest but was arrested by police before reaching her "target. They spotted her necklace with a cyanide capsule, a deadly decoration worn by Tamil terrorists in case of capture. Menake was beaten unconscious by police before she could swallow the pill.

M en and women become suicide bombers for complex reasons, but unless most are mentally ill, which is not the case, the common thread lies elsewhere. The culture of martyrdom among Tamil Tigers allows rape victims to redeem their outcast status with suicide bombings. Eternal salvation offers Islamic fundamentalists the same asymmetric payoff. None of this anecdotal evidence suggests that all female Tamil Tigers were raped. And not every Muslim suicide bomber believes in paradise. But the framework fits a wide spectrum of suicide bombers and explains the difficulty in stopping them, while also offering a clue to ending the practice.

The Sri Lankan government finally defeated the Tamil Tigers, showing them no mercy and ignoring the deadly fallout of its attack, just like the suicide bombers. In February 2009, after a two-year all-out war, government forces surrounded Tamil Tigers leaders along with their civilian supporters in the northeast coast of the country. The Sri Lankan Defense Secretary, Gotabaya Rajapaksa, who became the country's president in 2019, said, "The leaders are still there in that area, and they have that human shield. Very soon, when we overrun this place, we will be able to capture him [sic]."[31] The International Red Cross, estimating that 250,000 civilians were trapped in the combat zone and conceding that the Tamil Tigers would not let them leave, asked for a cease fire. Rajapaksa refused, explaining, "We have had so many cease fires in the last three decades. None of these cease fires solved the problem." He instructed his troops: "Do not give them any breathing space." Subsequent estimates put civilian deaths at more than 7,000.[32]

The *Los Angeles Times* suggested, "The tactics [Sri Lanka] used to defeat Tamil Tiger rebels could help other nations grappling with insurgencies," a ringing endorsement but a controversial tactic.[33] The UN criticized the Sri Lankan government for failing to protect innocent bystanders, despite evidence that many civilians caught in the crossfire sympathized with the rebels and abetted the terror. Indian military analyst Ajey Lele fingered the problem of following Sri Lanka: "They were not worried about collateral damage, so, in many respects, it's a very difficult model to adopt." Sri Lanka took a sledgehammer to the Tamil Tigers, a measure justified perhaps by decades of terror but branded as collective punishment and immoral by other countries.

Although collective punishment violates international law, it is routinely practiced in varying degrees by democracies throughout the world, according to Harvard law professor Alan Dershowitz: "Every time one nation retaliates against another, it collectively punishes the citizens of those countries. The American and British bombings of German cities [during World War II] punished the residents of those cities ... [and] there is collective economic punishment, such as UN-approved sanctions."[34] No bright dividing line separates acceptable collective punishment from the immoral, but democratic governments need a more nuanced weapon to deter suicide bombers—more like a scalpel than a sledgehammer.

Islamic fundamentalists and Tamil Tigers perceive an asymmetric payoff to their terror, but individuals in both groups want to please their families. For example, Murad Tawalbi, the would-be bomber from the West Bank, not only thanked his brother for helping him but also described how he and other recruits videotaped a final message: "Everybody says good-bye to their own family, so . . . when my mother hears on television that I have become a martyr, she will burst with joy and make cries of joy."[35] Knowing that suicide bombers care about their families means they have something to lose after all—an exploitable fissure in their armor.

Promising to demolish suicide bombers' family homes, for example, would hurt their loved ones, smooth the skewed payoff, and might force them to rethink their deadly decision.[36] In 1945 Britain began a policy of destroying family homes of suspected terrorists while administering the territory covered by the League of Nations Mandate for Palestine. Israel made extensive use of the practice during the first intifada, the Arab uprising against Israel that began in 1987, but abandoned it in 2005, partly because the international community condemned it as collective punishment—only to resume the penalty in response to an increase in terrorism in 2014.[37] A more palatable weapon would defer home demolition if a suicide bomber's parents publicly denounced their child's act. A parent's rebuke, videotaped to the world on social media, even if done under duress, carries weight and might counteract the asymmetric payoff more effectively than destroying a house, which can always be done if they recant.

No one knows if this combination would work. Two forces pull in opposite direction, like a tug-of-war. Islamic suicide bombers believe their faith promises paradise for their sacrifice, but they also care about their families. Although it is unlikely that the threat of destroying a home could outweigh paradise, stranger outcomes have prevailed. Few would have guessed that life-without-parole prisoners could be tamed by letting them show off at a rodeo, but that was the message of the last chapter. Do not underestimate the power of something to lose.

PART V

GETTING PERSONAL

CHAPTER 11

FREEDOM TO SUCCEED

"**F**reedom's just another word for nothin' left to lose," a line from a hit song penned by singer-songwriter Kris Kristofferson and performed by the blues and rock star Janis Joplin, could have been the theme of this book.[1] Freedom from restraint emboldens politicians and financiers to misbehave, causing collateral damage, like Hitler's futile Battle of the Bulge and Nick Leeson's destruction of Barings. But there is also a bright side: an unfettered spirit helps the downtrodden to advance a noble cause, such as Rosa Parks's Montgomery bus boycott. In the sports world, underdogs have taken that same idea to upset favored rivals, pleasing their beleaguered fans.

For example, on Saturday, November 10, 2007, the football team from West Virginia's Marshall University, with two wins and eight losses, clobbered the bowl-bound squad from East Carolina University, 26–7, as 26,718 smiling fans watched in amazement.[2] Byron Tinker, defensive tackle for the Thundering Herd, explained, "We didn't have anything to lose. We haven't been playing that way, but tonight we did. We were a lot freer. We had a lot more freedom. . . . And it showed during the game."[3]

The East Carolina football team lost to free-spirited Marshall perhaps because student-athletes are vulnerable, but even professionals can be victimized. The Denver Broncos won two Super Bowls in a row, following the 1997 and 1998 regular seasons, one of seven National Football League teams to have accomplished that feat. Over the next five years, the Broncos were good but not great, winning 53 percent of their regular-season games, but they were much better than the Chicago Bears, who won only 42 percent. The Broncos thought they were playoff bound in 2003, but on Sunday, November 23, the Bears arrived in Denver with three wins and seven losses, yet spanked the Broncos 19–10. A local sports column headlined "Broncos, Wake Up and Smell the Mediocrity."[4] Denver tight end Shannon Sharpe, a future Hall of Famer, explained what happened: "If you're playing a team that's seven and three, there's no way they go for it on all those fourth downs. But when you have the record they have, what do you have to lose? You don't have anything to lose, and that's the way they played. . . . They came in our backyard and beat us."

A carefree heart often spurs individual players to triumph. Evonne Goolagong grew up in the Australian outback, one of eight children in a poor Aborigine family, and became one of the greatest tennis stars in the world during the 1970s. Her first major victory came in early 1971 against her tennis idol, Margaret Court, a fellow Australian who won the Grand Slam of Tennis in 1970. Goolagong beat the older Court in the local Victorian championships, 7–6, 7–6, a stunning upset. Court was not pleased, saying after her defeat: "Evonne plays better against the top girls when she has nothing to lose."[5] Goolagong embraced the faint praise later in the year at Wimbledon, the British prize, when she beat U.S. star Billie Jean King, a three-time Wimbledon champion, in the semifinals. Evonne explained, "Things went for me out there. Everything came off. As I had nothing to lose, I had a go."[6] It was a winning formula for the budding superstar, and King complimented her, saying, "She was very kind to me out there. Tennis needs good young players like Evonne." Goolagong won Wimbledon that year just shy of her twentieth birthday, whipping Margaret Court, 6–4, 6–1, in the finals, a sweet victory.

Freedom from fear allows players to go for broke, winning when they least expect it, but a free spirit cannot sustain an athlete's career. Goolagong worried almost a decade later, "Wimbledon is more important to me now than when I won it. That year, everything was so new . . . and it didn't seem to be so important to me. . . . Now that tennis is more professional, and there's so much more involved in being a top player, it means more to me, and I'd really like to win it again before I stop."[7] She did, in 1980, a testament to her skill, but perhaps also to the spunk that comes with overcoming early challenges—an attitude that has advanced careers far from the athletic field.

Alan Dershowitz, born in Brooklyn in 1938, graduated first in his class from Yale Law School in 1962, clerked for Justice Arthur Goldberg of the U.S. Supreme Court, and became Harvard Law School's youngest full professor at age twenty-eight. An expert in U.S. constitutional law and an advocate of First Amendment rights, he has defended a number of high-profile—but questionable—clients, including Harry Reems, a pornographic movie star; Claus von Bülow, accused of attempting to murder his wife, socialite Sunny von Bülow; and O. J. Simpson, accused of murdering his ex-wife, Nicole Brown Simpson, and her friend Ron Goldman. Dershowitz also defended President Donald Trump during his 2020 Senate trial following his first impeachment by the House of Representatives.

Alan described his early school life to explain his penchant for being controversial: "I was a terrible student. I was always doubting, always asking questions, always trying to break out of what I thought was a closed system. I didn't do what they wanted me to do. . . . Risk taking always seemed natural to me."[8] He then added an asymmetric wrinkle to his calculus: "When I was young, I didn't have to conquer my fears because there was little at stake. I felt I had nothing to lose."

Richard M. Nixon, a lawyer by trade like Dershowitz, graduated third in his class from Duke University Law School and spent most of his adult life in political combat. He was vice president of the United States in both terms of the Eisenhower administration during the 1950s; ran for president against John F. Kennedy in 1960, and narrowly lost; then ran for governor of California in 1962 against Edmund "Pat" Brown, and lost. Nixon finally reached his life's goal by defeating Vice President Hubert Humphrey in the 1968 U.S. presidential election. After winning a second term in 1972, he resigned in humiliation two years later to avoid impeachment over the Watergate scandal.

Nixon explained that childhood insults drove him to excel: "What starts the process, really, are the laughs, slights, and snubs when you are a kid. Sometimes it's because you are poor, or Irish or Jewish or Catholic or ugly or simply that you are skinny. But if you are reasonably intelligent and if your anger is deep enough and strong enough, you learn you can change those attitudes by excellence, personal gut performance, while those who have anything are sitting on their fat butts."[9] He then described success: "Once you learn that you've got to work harder than anybody else, it becomes a way of life as you move out of the alley and on your way. In your own mind, you have nothing to lose, so you take plenty of chances, and if you do your homework, many of them pay off. It is then you understand, for the first time, that you really have the advantage because your competitors can't risk what they have already."

Nixon and Dershowitz had a lot to lose later in life, after they had reached the top, but both continued to gamble, perhaps because the strategy had worked. Dershowitz made it his life's calling, saying, "I love to win. I hate to lose. When I won the von Bülow appeal, my friends advised, 'Get out now.' They reasoned that if I lost the case, I'd be thought of as a loser. But I wanted to take the risk of losing. It's easy to win if you take easy cases. I only take high-risk cases."[10] Nixon pushed that attitude to excess: "So you are lean and mean and resourceful, and you continue to walk on the edge of the precipice because, over the years, you have become fascinated by how close to the edge you can walk without losing your balance." [11] And then he acknowledged paying the price with Watergate: "This time there was a difference. This time we had something to lose."

Sports teams, world-class athletes, superlawyers, and politicians have succeeded by taking chances, by pursuing outsize rewards, and by smothering fear of failure, almost like a racehorse wearing blinders. Their exploits have altered history, as we've seen throughout this book. But if opportunities with high upside and limited losses are so attractive, if they are the route to success, why don't we see more of them, and why don't Hail Marys dominate newspaper headlines? Reviewing how that ancient Roman Catholic prayer spread into daily conversation offers some insight.

Roger Staubach graduated from the U.S. Naval Academy, became a Pro Football Hall of Fame quarterback for the Dallas Cowboys, and led the team to two Super Bowl victories in the 1970s. He was known by various nicknames, including "Roger the Dodger," for his scrambling ability, and "Captain Comeback," for overcoming defeat in the fourth quarter of crucial games. The most memorable comeback occurred on Sunday, December 28, 1975, in a postseason contest. Dallas trailed the Minnesota Vikings 14–10, with only seconds remaining on the clock. Staubach then completed a fifty-yard heave to wide receiver Drew Pearson that won the game for the Cowboys, keeping them in the playoffs. Roger recalled the interview with reporters after the victory: "I was kidding around with the writers" and said "I got knocked down on the play. . . . I closed my eyes and said a Hail Mary."[12] He followed up: "It slowly became the term for anybody that was kind of in trouble." The National Football League sponsored T-shirts commemorating the phrase and made a customer of Staubach: "They have a big 'Hail Mary' on the front, and it explains the play on the back. I bought a bunch for my grandkids."

Roger Staubach was a great player and has contributed to American culture with the iconic phrase, but we remember only the winning tosses. In reality, few succeed.[13] No one discusses Staubach's failed Marys, but college football data show that quarterbacks threw 403 such passes between 2005 and 2013—almost 30 a year. Only 10 ended in touchdowns, a 2.5 percent success rate.[14] Most fall short because the defense prepares for the desperate gamble and usually prevents the lightning strike, but that has not stopped quarterbacks from trying to work that magic when the game is on the line. We just do not remember the failures.

A similar dynamic explains the scarcity of successful Hail Marys in politics, war, and business. They are, by definition, low-probability events, with the more numerous defeats gathering dust in history books. Few would remember that Eisenhower crushed Hitler's desperate gamble at the Battle of the Bulge, except for the killing field at Malmédy, and the 1965 film named *Battle of the Bulge,* starring Henry Fonda, Charles Bronson, and Telly Savalas, memorializing the story. Failed gambles disappear from the public record like losing thoroughbreds in the Kentucky Derby, but going for broke under duress occurs more often than we recall. For example, at least three presidential candidates in the United States in recent years wagered like Staubach when facing defeat, choosing unconventional running mates to boost their chances. Two surprises were women, but not the third. Do you remember them all?

The most recent candidate to roll the dice was Republican John McCain, who chose the little-known governor of Alaska, Sarah Palin, as his vice president after polls during the summer of 2008 predicted victory for Democrat Barack Obama. A headline in the press read, "McCain's Hail Mary Pass."[15] An Alaska delegate to the Republican convention, Bill Noll, said, "If this doesn't resonate with every woman in America, I'll eat my hat." He probably choked on his fedora when the Republicans lost decisively. But Palin was not the first woman selected as a vice presidential candidate on a major party ticket. That honor belongs to Democratic congresswoman Geraldine Ferraro of New York, picked by Walter Mondale in his 1984 failed bid to unseat President Ronald Reagan. *Boston Globe* syndicated columnist Ellen Goodman wrote, "The choice of the first woman was one-part inspiration, one-part perspiration, one-part desperation. . . . Ferraro was the walking, talking 'Hail Mary pass' in the race against the Gipper."[16] The third big gamble occurred in 1996, when Republican senator Robert Dole, a former vice presidential candidate in 1976, tried to unseat President Bill Clinton in his reelection bid. National polls put Dole 20 points behind Clinton during the summer of 1996 when the senator chose his running mate, New York congressman Jack Kemp, a former star quarterback of the Buffalo Bills.

Kemp had won the American Football League's Most Valuable Player Award in 1965, retired from the NFL in 1970, and overcame the dumb-jock label by studying economics and pushing tax cuts in Congress to jump-start the economy. Nevertheless, when Dole announced his choice, Democrats highlighted the desperation by giving out miniature footballs carrying the words "Hail Mary Pass."[17] In a brief history of vice presidential picks, *Time* magazine wrote: "Those still shaking their heads in puzzlement over John McCain's veep choice in 2008 have short memories: before there was Sarah Palin, there was Jack Kemp."[18]

A nothing-to-lose attitude might make you a tennis star like Evonne Goolagong or a superlawyer like Alan Dershowitz, but prepare for a bumpy ride because success requires more than just a lucky roll of the dice. In 1997 a teenager with braces on her teeth, who had practiced on shabby public courts, surprised everyone by reaching the finals of the U.S. Open Tennis Tournament in Flushing Meadows, New York. A victory would be the first by an unseeded woman—unprecedented, like Amelia Earhart's solo flight across the Atlantic in 1932. But Martina Hingis, ranked number one in the world, stood in the way with a powerful mantra: "The best feeling you can have out there is knowing that no one is better than you."[19] Hingis added a touch of disrespect for her opponent, calling Venus Williams "just another player who has nothing to lose."

The seventeen-year-old Williams had that magic incentive in 1997 but fell short. Martina beat her in the finals, 6–0, 6–4, because she was the better player at the time. But not for long. Venus shook off that defeat and won the U.S. Open in 2000 and 2001, the same years she won at Wimbledon, and would go on to three more victories at the All England Club. Venus Williams would dominate the sport with her younger sister, Serena, during the first decade of the twenty-first century, but injuries and illness would take their toll.

Venus was diagnosed with Sjogren's syndrome in 2011, an autoimmune disease that produces dry eyes, dry mouth, and fatigue, not ideal for the tennis tour. She said, "You just get diagnosed when you have the symptoms. It took a long time."[20] Williams added, "So, on a daily basis, I try to get the best out of myself. That's all I can ask." In June 2014, at age thirty-four, ranked thirty-first in the world, she entered Wimbledon with little hope but made it to the third round. Pleased with her performance, she explained how she got that far: "Trying to conserve is not the right mentality. You have to go out there and give it your all, and just play smart." And then she said, "I have nothing to prove, nothing to hide, nothing to lose."

A complete recipe.

ACKNOWLEDGMENTS

I would like to thank my NYU Stern students who participated over the years in the stock-picking contest that is the underlying theme of this book. It was an idea sparked by my friend and former teaching assistant David Stonberg, who suggested including a current events project in my course. A number of my colleagues read this manuscript at various stages, including Kenneth Garbade, Dick Sylla, and Bruce Tuckman. They caught mistakes in numerous places that would have embarrassed me. Too bad they did not catch them all. My agent, Richard Abate, and my adviser, Claire Wachtel, pushed me to expand the discussions beyond my comfort zone, making my task more difficult but enhancing the final product. The very wise Mauro DiPreta, my editor, understood the big picture and also paid attention to details. He brought the book to a different level of sophistication. My wife, Lillian, read every word of every chapter, adding a compassionate perspective, and my children and grandchildren listened to my descriptions as though they were really interested. I also want to thank my good friend Tom Sargent—a humble Nobel Prize winner—for his encouragement at the very beginning. They all get partial credit for the final product and perhaps deserve a share of the blame as well.

NOTES

CHAPTER 1   DOWNSIDE PROTECTION

1.   The story that follows was reported in many newspapers. The facts are drawn from the following two accounts: Melissa Gomez and Julia Jacobs, "Texas Man's Near-Fatal Lesson: A Decapitated Snake Can Still Bite," *New York Times,* June 8, 2018, A15, and Allyson Chiu, "A Texas Man Decapitated a Rattlesnake. It Bit Him Anyway and He Nearly Died, His Wife Says," *Washington Post* online, June 7, 2018, https://www.washingtonpost.com/news/morning-mix/wp/2.

2.   Gomez and Jacobs, "Near-Fatal Lesson," A15.

3.   Ibid.

4.   This quote and the information in this paragraph come from Simona Kralj-Fiser et al., "Eunuchs Are Better Fighters," *Animal Behavior* 81 (2011): 933–39. See also John Barrat, "Don't Pick a Fight with a Eunuch Spider. It Has Nothing to Lose," Animals, Research News, Science & Nature, Smithsonian Insider, April 7, 2011, https://insider.si.edu/2011/04/dont-pick-a-fight-with-a-eunuch-spider-its-got-nothing-to-lose/.

5.   Peter King, "I Desperately Want to Be Coached," *Sports Illustrated* online, September 9, 2015, https://www.si.com/mmqb/2015/09/09/aaron-rodgers-mike-mccarthy-tom-clements-green-back-packers-avoiding-interceptions.

6.   See "NFL Career Leaders—Passing Touchdown/Interception Ratio," Football Database, https://www.footballdb.com/leaders/career-passing-tdintratio.

7. John C. Fitzpatrick, ed., *The Writings of George Washington from the Original Manuscript Sources, 1745–1799*, vol. 4, *October, 1775–April, 1776* (Washington, D.C.: Government Printing Office, 1932), 209.

8. Ibid., 392.

9. John C. Fitzpatrick, ed., *The Writings of George Washington from the Original Manuscript Sources, 1745–1799*, vol. 6, *September, 1776–January, 1777* (Washington, D.C.: Government Printing Office, 1932), 347.

10. Ibid.

11. Ibid., 401–2.

12. Ibid., 436.

13. See Philip K. Gray and Stephen F. Gray, "Testing Market Efficiency: Evidence from the NFL Sports Betting Market," *Journal of Finance* 52, no. 4 (September 1997): 1725–37, and Steven D. Levitt, "Why Are Gambling Markets Organized So Differently from Financial Markets?," *Economic Journal* 114, no. 495 (April 2004): 223–46.

14. For a detailed summary of the 1969 Super Bowl story, see Jack Doyle, "I Guarantee It. Joe Namath," PopHistoryDig.com, November 18, 2020, http://www.pophistorydig.com/topics/joe-namath.

15. Larry Cao, "Nobel Laureate Myron Scholes on the Black-Scholes Option Pricing Model," Enterprising Investor, October 13, 2014, https://blogs.cfainstitute.org/investor/2014/10/13/nobel-laureate -myron-scholes-on-the-black-scholes-option-pricing-model. See also Fischer Black and Myron Scholes, "The Pricing of Options and Corporate Liabilities," *Journal of Political Economy* 81, no. 3 (May/June 1973): 637–54.

16. See Jared Diamond, "The Best Young Player in Baseball Swings on 3-0. Here's Why Everyone Should," *Wall Street Journal*, August 21, 2020, A12.

17. Ibid.

18. Charles V. P. von Luttichau, "The German Counteroffensive in the Ardennes," chap. 20 in *Command Decisions* (Washington, D.C.: Center

of Military History, U.S. Army, 1960), 444, available at Hathi Trust Digital Library, https://catalog.hathitrust.org/Record/011414502.

19. Ibid.

20. These are the last lines of chap. 4 of the *Manifesto of the Communist Party,* before the final phrase "Working Men of All Countries, Unite." See Karl Marx and Frederick Engels, *Marx/Engels Selected Works,* vol. 1 (Moscow: Progress Publishers, 1969), 98–137, available at Marxists Internet Archive, https://www.marxists.org/archive /marx/works/download/pdf/Manifesto.pdf.

21. Donald Trump with Tony Schwartz, *The Art of the Deal* (New York: Ballantine Books Trade Paperback, 2015), 48.

22. The probabilities vary, depending on where the throw starts. For some estimates, see Brian Burke, "Hail Mary Probabilities," Advanced Football Analytics, September 25, 2012, http://archive .advancedfootballanalytics.com/2012/09/hail-mary-probabilities .html, and "Hail Marys—Just How Improbable Are They?," CougarStats, last modified September 10, 2015, https://blog.cougarstats .com/2015/09/10/hail-marys-just-how-improbable-are-they/.

23. Maureen Dowd, "Manic Panic on the Potomac," *New York Times,* October 11, 2020, SR9.

CHAPTER 2   LAME-DUCK U.S. PRESIDENTS

1. Even Eisenhower suffered the indignity of forcing the resignation of his chief of staff, Sherman Adams, accused of influence peddling in 1958, two years into the thirty-fourth president's second term in office. But no one accused Eisenhower of doing anything illegal.

2. Harold Ickes, *The Secret Diary of Harold L. Ickes: The First Thousand Days, 1933–1936* (New York: Simon & Schuster, 1953), 274.

3. Jamie L. Carson and Benjamin A. Kleinerman, "A Switch in Time Saves Nine: Institutions, Strategic Actors, and FDR's Court-Packing Plan," *Public Choice* 113, nos. 3 and 4 (December 2002): 303.

4.   "President's Message," *New York Times,* February 6, 1937, 1.

5.   "Bar Head Attacks Court Proposal," *New York Times,* February 6, 1937, 9.

6.   Ibid.

7.   "Opinions of the Nation's Press on Court Plan," *New York Times,* February 6, 1937, 10.

8.   A broad index of the stock market, the S&P 500, declined by 1.6 percent that day, and the daily standard deviation of returns over the previous ninety calendar days was .87 percent.

9.   "Stocks Drop Fast on Court Message," *New York Times,* February 6, 1937, 1.

10. Quoted in National Constitution Center staff, "How FDR Lost His Brief War on the Supreme Court," *Constitution Daily,* February 5, 2020, available at https://constitutioncenter.org/blog/how-fdr-lost -his-brief-war-on-the-supreme-court-2.

11. See discussion of John Nance Garner at United States Senate, available at "John Nance Garner," Art and History, United States Senate, https://www.senate.gov/artandhistory/art/artifact/Painting _31_00007.htm.

12. See Colleen Shogan, "The Contemporary Presidency: The Sixth Year Curse," *Presidential Studies Quarterly* 36, no. 1 (March 2006): 96, for the suggestion of overconfidence. She does not mention downside protection.

13. An excellent biography of Calvin Coolidge is Amity Shlaes, *Coolidge* (New York: HarperCollins, 2013).

14. This quote and the next are from "President Wilson Bids All His Countrymen Be Neutral Both in Speech and Action," *Christian Science Monitor,* August 18, 1914, 1.

15. Two books provide detailed information on the RMS *Lusitania:* Douglas C. Peifer, *Choosing War: Presidential Decisions in the* Maine, Lusitania, *and* Panay *Incidents* (New York: Oxford University Press,

2016), and Erik Larson, *Dead Wake: The Last Crossing of the* Lusitania (New York: Crown, 2015).

16. "Press Calls Sinking of Lusitania Murder," *New York Times*, May 8, 1915, 6.

17. "President Drafting Policy for Cabinet," *Boston Daily Globe*, May 9, 1915, 1.

18. "A. G. Vanderbilt's Career Is Very Spectacular," *San Francisco Chronicle*, May 9, 1915, 32.

19. "Owners Believed the *Lusitania* Could Not Be Sunk: Her Construction Was Better Than the *Titanic*,"*Los Angeles Times*, May 8, 1915, 19.

20. See Bruno S. Frey, David A. Savage, and Benno Torgler, "Behavior Under Extreme Conditions: The Titanic Disaster," *Journal of Economic Perspectives* 25, no. 1 (Winter 2011): 218, table 3.

21. This description is based primarily on "Germany Admits Torpedoing *Lusitania*; 'Let Them Think,' Bernstorff's Comment; American Dead 115; Children, 25," *New York Tribune*, May 9, 1915, 1.

22. Some eyewitnesses thought a second torpedo had hit, but the most recent evidence points to the rush of cold seawater against a boiler that caused the second explosion. See Peifer, *Choosing War*, 85–87.

23. See ibid., 73.

24. "Passengers Too Confident," *New York Times*, May 10, 1915, 3.

25. This paragraph is based on Peifer, *Choosing War*, 73–74, and Larson, *Dead Wake*, 259–60.

26. The quotes in this paragraph are from "How the Great Ship Went Down," *Weekly Irish Times*, May 15, 1915, 3.

27. Ibid.

28. See Peifer, *Choosing War*, 73–74, and Larson, *Dead Wake*, 259–60.

29. "Wilson Calmly Considers," *New York Times*, May 10, 1915, 1.

30. Woodrow Wilson,"Address to Naturalized Citizens at Convention Hall, Philadelphia," May 10, 1915, available at American Presidency Project,

https://www.presidency.ucsb.edu/documents/address-naturalized
-citizens-convention-hall-philadelphia.

31. The quotes in this paragraph are from "Crime of Ages, Colonel Says," *Chicago Daily Tribune,* May 12, 1915, 1.

32. Mark Benhow, review of *Colonel House: A Biography of Woodrow Wilson's Silent Partner,* by Charles E. Neu (New York: Oxford University Press, 2014), Central Intelligence Agency online, Intelligence in Public Media, September 28, 2015, https://www.cia.gov/library/center-for-the-study-of-intelligence/csi-publications/csi-studies/studies/vol-59-no-3/colonel-house.html.

33. Edward Mandell House, *The Intimate Papers of Colonel House: From Neutrality to War, 1915–1917,* vol. 1, ed. Charles Seymour (Boston: Houghton Mifflin, 1926), 434.

34. Larson, *Dead Wake,* 281.

35. The original text of the diplomatic note appears in the *Los Angeles Times,* May 14, 1915, 12, and a summary in layman's terms appears in "Leading Points In President's Note to Germany Demanding Redress for Attack on Americans," *New York Times,* May 13, 1915, 1.

36. The quotations in this paragraph come from William G. McAdoo, *Crowded Years: The Reminiscences of William G. McAdoo* (Boston: Houghton Mifflin, 1931), 366–67.

37. Edward Mandell House, *The Intimate Papers of Colonel House: From Neutrality to War, 1915–1917,* vol. 2, ed. Charles Seymour (Boston: Houghton Mifflin, 1926), 239.

38. Ibid., 341 and 347.

39. Ibid., 359–60.

40. "Kansas Lead Piles Up for President Wilson," *Chicago Daily Tribune,* November 9, 1916, 4.

41. "Votes of Women and Bull Moose Elected Wilson," *New York Times,* November 12, 1916, 1.

42. "Wilson Solid with California Women," *Boston Daily Globe,* November 9, 1916, 10.

43. The twelve states granting women the right to vote in the 1916 presidential elections were Wyoming, Colorado, Utah, Idaho, Washington, California, Arizona, Kansas, Oregon, Montana, Nevada, and Illinois. All but Oregon and Illinois voted for Wilson. See *Map: States Grant Women the Right to Vote (January 1, 1919),* "Centuries of Citizenship: A Constitutional Timeline," National Constitution Center online, https://constitutioncenter.org/timeline/html/cw08_12159 .html.

44. This quote and the next two are from House, *Intimate Papers of Colonel House,* vol. 2, 390–91.

45. "Foreign Issues Faced," *Washington Post,* November 20, 1916, 1.

46. "A Ship a Week for US," *New York Times,* February 1, 1917, 1.

47. "Germany Asks Mexico to Seek Alliance with Japan for War on U.S.," *New York Tribune,* March 1, 1917, 1.

48. The quote is from Larson, *Dead Wake,* 340.

49. The quotes in this paragraph and the next are from "Text of the President's Address," *New York Times,* April 3, 1917, 1, and from "Must Exert All Our Power," *New York Times,* April 3, 1917, 1.

50. "Must Exert All Our Power," *New York Times,* April 3, 1917, 1.

51. "For Freedom and Civilization," editorial, *New York Times,* April 3, 1917, 12.

52. Larson, *Dead Wake,* 343.

CHAPTER 3   PARDON ME

1. William F. Duker, "The President's Power to Pardon," *William & Mary Law Review* 18, no. 3 (March 1977): 479.

2. A list of nine murders committed by freed or escaped murderers appears in appendix A in Paul J. Larkin Jr., "The Demise of Capital Clemency," *Washington and Lee Law Review* 73, no. 3 (Summer 2016): 350–51.

3. Laura Argys and Naci Mocan, "Who Shall Live and Who Shall Die: An Analysis of Prisoners on Death Row in the United States," *Journal of Legal Studies* 33, no. 2 (June 2004): 255–82.

4. United Press International, "Lame Duck Gov. Blanton Frees Killer, Son of Crony," *Los Angeles Times,* January 16, 1979, A2, and Associated Press, "Governor Shocks Tennessee with Clemency for 52," *Chicago Tribune,* January 17, 1979, 2.

5. Associated Press, "Gov. Blanton Sets 8 Murderers Free," *Los Angeles Times,* January 17, 1979, B28.

6. Howell Raines, "Gov. Blanton of Tennessee Is Replaced 3 Days Early in Pardons Dispute," *New York Times,* January 18, 1979, A16.

7. Associated Press, "Blanton Sets 8 Murderers Free," B28.

8. The *Philadelphia Inquirer* (April 11, 1979, 3A) reported that the Tennessee appeals court upheld the last-minute grants.

9. Eleanor Randolph, "Blanton: Tennessee's Hillbilly Nixon," *Chicago Tribune,* January 21, 1979, B14.

10. Ray Hill, "Ray Blanton, Part 5," *Knoxville Focus* online, January 22, 2017, http://knoxfocus.com/archives/this-weeks-focus/ray-blanton -part-5/.

11. This quote and the next are from Randolph, "Hillbilly Nixon," B14.

12. For this fact and the remaining points in this paragraph, see Campbell Robertson, "Mississippi Governor, Already Criticized on Pardons, Rides a Wave of Them out of Office," *New York Times,* January 11, 2012, A13.

13. The examples in this paragraph are from Campbell Robertson and Stephanie Saul, "List of Pardons Included Many Tied to Power," *New York Times* online, January 27, 2012, https://www.nytimes

.com/2012/01/28/us/many-pardon-applicants-stressed-connection
-to-mississippi-governor.html, and Linda Killian, "Haley Barbour's Last-
Minute Pardons Hurt the GOP's Law and Order Image," Daily Beast,
January 18, 2012, https://www.thedailybeast.com/haley-barbours-last
-minute-pardons-hurt-the-gops-law-and-order-image.

14. "Editorial: Furthermore . . ." *Journal-Gazette* (Fort Wayne, IN), January 14, 2012, A10.

15. Robertson, "Mississippi Governor," A13. The quote is from "Mississippi Judge Blocks Release of Pardoned Prisoners," *St. Joseph (MO)
News-Press,* January 11, 2012.

16. Emily Le Coz, "Barbour Pardons One Year Later: What 'Life' Looks
Like," *Clarion Ledger* (Jackson, MS) January 13, 2013, 3C–6C.

17. This quote and the next are from Amy Goldstein and Susan Schmidt,
"Clinton's Last Day Clemency Benefits 176; List Includes Pardons for
Cisneros, McDougal, Deutsch, and Roger Clinton," *Washington Post,*
January 21, 2001, A1.

18. From Weston Kosova, "Backstage at the Finale," *Newsweek,* February
26, 2001, 30–35.

19. This quote and the remaining discussion in this paragraph are from ibid.

20. Goldstein and Schmidt, "Clinton's Last Day Clemency Benefits
176," A1.

21. Margaret Colgate Love, "The Pardon Paradox: Lessons of Clinton's
Last Pardons," *Capital University Law Review* 32, no. 1 (2002): 210.

22. Goldstein and Schmidt, "Clinton's Last Day Clemency Benefits
176," A1.

23. "The Controversial Pardon of International Fugitive Marc Rich,"
*Hearings Before the Committee on Government Reform, House of Repre-
sentatives, One Hundred Seventh Congress, First Session, February 8, and
March 1, 2001* (Washington, D.C.: U.S. Government Printing Office, 2001), 102–3, https://www.govinfo.gov/content/pkg/CHRG
-107hhrg75593/html/CHRG-107hhrg75593.htm.

24. This quote and the information in this paragraph are from Albert W. Alschuler, "Bill Clinton's Parting Pardon Party," *Journal of Criminal Law and Criminology* 100, no. 3 (Summer 2010), 1140.

25. Ibid., 1141.

26. See letter dated February 7, 2001, from the lawyer representing Denise Rich to committee chairman Dan Burton asserting her Fifth Amendment right not to testify, in "Controversial Pardon of International Fugitive Marc Rich," 3.

27. "Controversial Pardon of International Fugitive Marc Rich," 106–7.

28. The quotes in this paragraph are from "An Indefensible Pardon," editorial, *New York Times,* January 24, 2001, A18; "Unpardonable," *Washington Post,* January 23, 2001, A16; "A Paid Pardon?" *Christian Science Monitor,* January 25, 2001, 10.

29. E. J. Dionne Jr., "And the Gifts That Keep on Giving," *Washington Post,* February 6, 2001, 17.

30. This quote and the next in this paragraph are from Glen Johnson, "Frank Seeks Ban on End-of-Term Pardons," *Boston Globe,* February 28, 2001, A8.

31. Gregory Sisk, "Suspending the Pardon Power During the Twilight of a Presidential Term," *Missouri Law Review* 67, no. 1 (Winter 2002).

32. This quote and the next are from Reuters, "The Pardons: Independent Counsel's Statement on the Pardons," *New York Times,* December 25, 1992, 22.

33. Sisk, "Suspending the Pardon Power," 23.

34. "Pardons Granted by President Barack Obama (2009–2017)," U.S. Department of Justice online, July 11, 2018, https://www.justice.gov/pardon/obama-pardons.

35. The quotes are from Clark Hoyt, "Ford's Burial of Watergate Only Revives It," *Philadelphia Inquirer,* September 11, 1974, 5, and "The Failure of Mr. Ford," editorial, *New York Times,* September 9, 1974, 34.

36. This quote and the next are from Linda Mathews, "Aide Says Ford Won't Grant Pardon If Nixon Is Prosecuted," *Los Angeles Times,* August 11, 1974, 1.

37. See Mitchell Lynch and Albert Hunt, "Ford Pardons Nixon; Move on Watergate Jolts His Honeymoon," *Wall Street Journal,* September 9, 1974, 1.

38. Warren Weaver Jr., "Cox's Ouster Ruled Illegal; No Reinstatement Ordered," *New York Times,* November 15, 1973, 1.

39. Chris Cillizza, "Donald Trump's 'Pardon' Tweet Tells Us a Lot About Where His Head Is At," CNN online, June 4, 2018, https://www.cnn.com/2018/06/04/politics/donald-trump-tweet-pardon/index.html.

40. Adam Liptak, "Supreme Court Rules Trump Cannot Block Release of Financial Records," *New York Times* online, July 9, 2020, https://www.nytimes.com/2020/07/09/us/trump-taxes-supreme-court.html?searchResultPosition=1.

41. Garrett Epps, "Can Trump Pardon Himself?," *Atlantic* online, December 17, 2018, https://www.theatlantic.com/ideas/archive/2018/12/can-trump-pardon-himself/578074/.

42. Philip Bump, "Could Trump Issue Himself a Pardon?," *Washington Post* online, May 24, 2017, https://www.washingtonpost.com/news/politics/wp/2017/05/24/could-trump-issue-himself-a-pardon/.

43. Details in this paragraph on the state pardon arrangements are from Kristen H. Fowler, "Limiting the Federal Pardon Power," *Indiana Law Journal* 83, no. 4 (Fall 2008): 1661ff.

CHAPTER 4 ASYLUM SEEKERS

1. This story and the quote are from Boryana Dzhambazova, "Facebook's Group Push for Safe Land Passage for Migrants Founders," *New York Times* online, September 19, 2015, https://www.nytimes.com/2015/09/20/world/facebook-groups-push-for-safe-land-passage-for-migrants-founders.html.

2. This quote and the others in this paragraph are from "On the Road to Sanctuary," *Washington Post,* September 8, 2015, A8.

3. Patrick Kinglsey, "Is Trump's America Tougher on Asylum Than Other Western Countries?," *New York Times* online, September 14, 2019, https://www.nytimes.com/2019/09/14/world/europe/trump -america-asylum-migration.html?searchResultPosition=1.

4. This quote and the next are from Dzhambazova, "Facebook's Group Push for Safe Land Passage."

5. Kirk Bansak, Jens Hainmueller, and Dominik Hangartner, "How Economic, Humanitarian, and Religious Concerns Shape European Attitudes Toward Asylum Seekers," *Science* 354, no. 6309 (October 14, 2016): 217–22.

6. Kim Hjelmgaard, "Trump Isn't the Only One Who Wants to Build a Wall. These European Nations Already Did," *USA Today* online, May 24, 2018, https://www.usatoday.com/story/news/world/2018/05/24 /donald-trump-europe-border-walls-migrants/532572002.

7. This sentence and the next are based on Joshua J. Mark, "Hadrian's Wall," Ancient History Encyclopedia, November 15, 2012, https:// www.ancient.eu/Hadrians_Wall.

8. Thanks to my friend Ken Garbade for this example. See Keith Ray, "A Brief History of Offa's Dyke," HistoryExtra, April 25, 2016, https://www.historyextra.com/period/anglo-saxon/a-brief-history -of-offas-dyke.

9. See Ran Abramitzky and Leah Boustan, "Immigration in American Economic History," *Journal of Economic Literature* 55, no. 4 (December 2017): 1311–45.

10. Ibid.

11. "Historical Highlights: The Immigration Act of 1924," U.S. House of Representatives History, Art & Archives, https://history .house.gov/Historical-Highlights/1901-1950/The-Immigration -Act-of-1924.

12. "The Immigration Act of 1924 (The Johnson-Reed Act)," U.S. Department of State Office of the Historian online, https://history .state.gov/milestones/1921-1936/immigration-act.

13. Kristofer Allerfeldt, "'And We Got Here First': Albert Johnson, National Origins and Self-Interest in the Immigration Debate of the 1920s," *Journal of Contemporary History* 45, no. 1 (January 2010): 20.

14. This quote defines the term *refugee* according to the UN document *Convention and Protocol Relating to the Status of Refugees* (Geneva: United Nations High Commissioner for Refugees, December 2010), 14, https://www.unhcr.org/en-us/protection/basic/3b66c2aa10 /convention-protocol-relating-status-refugees.html.

15. Ronda Robinson, "Survivor of the Voyage of the Damned," Aish Hatorah Holocaust Studies, October 8, 2015, https://www.aish .com/ho/p/Survivor-of-the-Voyage-of-the-Damned.html.

16. See Ian McShane, "Voyage of the Damned: MV St. Louis," *Sea Classics* 45, no. 1 (January 2012): 18.

17. The details in this paragraph are from R. Hart Phillips, "Cuba Orders Liner and Refugees to Go," *New York Times,* June 1, 1939, 1, and "Refugees Returning to Reich as All Doors Close; Final Appeals to Cuba," *Jewish Advocate,* June 9, 1939, 1.

18. Robinson, "Survivor of the Voyage of the Damned."

19. George Axelsson, "907 Refugees End Voyage in Antwerp," *New York Times,* June 18, 1939, 1.

20. R. Hart Phillips, "907 Refugees Quit Cuba on Liner; Ship Reported Hovering off Coast," *New York Times,* June 3, 1939, 1, and Associated Press, "Refugee Liner Cruising About Florida Coast," *Boston Globe,* June 5, 1939, 1.

21. Associated Press, "Ship Sails Back with 907 Jews Who Fled Nazis," *Chicago Daily Tribune,* June 7, 1939, 12.

22. Amy Tikkanen, "MS St. Louis: German Ocean Liner," *Encyclopedia Britannica* online, https://www.britannica.com/topic/MS-St-Louis-German-ship.

23. James Besser, "Exploring 'Ship of the Damned,'" *Jewish Week* online, April 16, 1999, https://jewishweek.timesofisrael.com/exploring-ship-of-the-damned.

24. "The Righteous Among the Nations: Gustave Schroeder," Yad Vashem (the World Holocaust Remembrance Center) online, https://www.yadvashem.org/righteous/stories/schroeder.html.

25. The number of passengers from the *St. Louis* murdered in the Holocaust is from Tikkanen, "MS St. Louis: German Ocean Liner."

26. See Associated Press, "Refugee Liner Cruising About Florida," 1.

27. See "Refugees Returning to Reich," 1.

28. Besser, "Exploring 'Ship of the Damned.'"

29. See "States Parties to the 1951 Convention Relating to the Status of Refugees and the 1967 Protocol," United Nations High Commissioner for Refugees (UNHCR) online, April 2015, https://www.unhcr.org/protect/PROTECTION/3b73b0d63.pdf.

30. The details in this paragraph and the next are based on Griff Witte, "In Heart of Europe, Migrants Offer a One-Stop Tour of Worldwide Misery," *Washington Post* online, November 27, 2014, https://www.washingtonpost.com/world/europe/in-heart-of-europe-migrants-offer-a-one-stop-tour-of-worldwide-misery/2014/11/26/cff5fc3e-5933-11e4-9d6c-756a229d8b18_story.html.

31. Ibid.

32. Ibid.

33. The details in this paragraph are based on Craig R. Whitney, "Human Tides: The Influx in Europe—A Special Report. Europeans Look for Ways to Bar Door to Immigrants," *New York Times,* December 29, 1991, A1.

34. Ibid.

35. Ibid.

36. See James Traub, "The Death of the Most Generous Nation on Earth," *Foreign Policy* online, February 20, 2016, https://foreignpolicy .com/2016/02/10/the-death-of-the-most-generous-nation-on-earth -sweden-syria-refugee-europe/.

37. This quote and the next are from ibid.

38. "Australia's Refugee Problem," editorial, *New York Times* online, July 4, 2014, https://www.nytimes.com/2014/07/05/opinion/australias -refugee-problem.html?searchResultPosition=1.

39. "Australia Sends Asylum-Seekers to Nauru, as India Offer Refused," *Economic Times* online, August 2, 2014, https://economictimes.india times.com/news/politics-and-nation/australia-sends-asylum -seekers-to-nauru-as-india-offer-refused/articleshow/39469692.cms.

40. "Australia's Refugee Problem," editorial.

41. This quote and the next are from Lloyd Jones, "Amnesty Slams Australian Boat Turn-Back Policy," EFE News Service online, June 13, 2017, https://www.efe.com/efe/english/world/amnesty-slams -australian-boat-turn-back-policy/50000262-3294519.

42. Craig Furini, "Return of 13 Potential Illegal Immigrants to Sri Lanka" (transcript), Australian Government Operation Sovereign Borders online, https://osb.homeaffairs.gov.au/#.

43. Details of the dinner are from Michael Collins, "After a Rocky Start with the Aussies, Donald Trump Hosts State Dinner for PM Scott Morrison," *USA Today* online, September 20, 2019, https://www.usa today.com/story/news/politics/2019/09/20/state-dinner-trump -hosts-australian-prime-minister-scott-morrison/2344441001/.

44. The full transcript of the toast is available at Nina Zafar and Caitlin Moore, "Full Transcript: The Toasts of President Trump and Prime Minister Scott Morrison at the State Dinner for Australia," *Washington Post* online, September 20, 2019, https://www.washingtonpost.com /arts-entertainment/2019/09/21/full-transcript-toasts-president -trump-prime-minister-scott-morrison-state-dinner-australia.

45. This quote and the next are from Luke Henriques-Gomes, "Donald Trump Says 'Much Can Be Learned' from Australia's Hardline Asylum Seeker Policies," *Guardian* (U.S. edition) online, June 27, 2019, https://www.theguardian.com/us-news/2019/jun/27/donald-trump-says -much-can-be-learned-from-australias-hardline-asylum-seeker-policies.

46. "Prime Minister Snags Stunning Election Win on 'Quiet Australians,'" *New York Times,* May 19, 2019, A8.

47. Russell Goldman and Damien Cave, "U.N. Sees 'Emergency' in the Pacific," *New York Times,* November 3, 2017, A9.

48. This quote and the next are from Damien Cave, "A Timeline of Despair in Australia's Offshore Detention Centers," *New York Times* online, June 26, 2019, https://www.nytimes.com/2019/06/26/world /australia/australia-manus-suicide.html?searchResultPosition=1.

49. Ibid.

50. This discussion and the remaining quotes are from Shahram Khosravi, "Sweden: Detention and Deportation of Asylum Seekers," *Race & Class* 50, no. 4 (2009): 38–56.

51. Didier Fassin and Estelle d'Halluin, "The Truth from the Body: Medical Certificates as Ultimate Evidence for Asylum Seekers," *American Anthropologist* 107, no. 4 (December 2005): 600.

52. Ibid., 599.

53. The data on applications to the EU are from "Eurostat Statistics Explained: Asylum Statistics," European Commission online, September 2, 2020, https://ec.europa.eu/eurostat/statistics-explained /index.php/Asylum_statistics.

54. This quote and the rest in this paragraph are from Sally Kestin and Tom Collie, "Flight from Poverty: Many Share the View of a Grand Bahama Human Rights Association Secretary; 'When You Have Nothing, You Have Nothing to Lose,'" *South Florida Sun-Sentinel,* November 3, 2002, 1A.

55. Ibid.

CHAPTER 5   ROSA PARKS

1. Josh Moon, "Bus Boycott Took Planning, Smarts," *Montgomery (AL) Advertiser* online, November 29, 2015, https://www.montgomery advertiser.com/story/news/local/blogs/moonblog/2015/11/29 /bus-boycott-took-planning-smarts/76456904.

2. Burt Wade Cole, "Parks Recalls '55 Bus Protest," *Hartford (CT) Courant,* July 15, 1984, H10E.

3. In December 2020, Fred Gray, age ninety, was honored with a proposal by the mayor of Montgomery to rename a street for him. See Elaina Plott, "For a Civil Rights Hero, 90, a New Battle Unfolds on His Childhood Street," *New York Times,* December 26, 2020, A1.

4. The portrait of Fred Gray comes from "Alabama Bus Boycotters Sing 'My Country Tis of Thee,'" *Baltimore Afro-American,* February 11, 1956, A1.

5. Fred Gray, *Bus Ride to Justice: Changing the System by the System* (Montgomery, AL: New South Books, 1995), 5.

6. This quote and the remaining in this paragraph are from "Tired of Being Treated like Dogs," *Baltimore Afro-American,* March 31, 1956, 6.

7. This quote and the next are from "Why Do We Have to Get Kicked Around?," *Baltimore Afro-American,* May 26, 1956, 19.

8. "People, Places, and Things," *Chicago Defender,* April 2, 1955, 8.

9. The quote is from Gray, *Bus Ride to Justice,* 47.

10. The name Mr. Civil Rights is from ibid., 28.

11. Rosa Parks with Jim Haskins, *Rosa Parks: My Story* (New York: Puffin, 1999), 73.

12. Gray, *Bus Ride to Justice,* 28.

13. This version of the decision not to proceed with Claudette Colvin follows Jeanne Theoharis, *The Rebellious Life of Mrs. Rosa Parks* (Boston: Beacon Press, 2013), 57. Rosa Parks (Parks with Haskins,

Rosa Parks, 112) writes, "Everything was going along fine until Mr. Nixon discovered that Claudette was pregnant." Theoharis (fifty-eight) claims that revelation occurred after Nixon made the negative decision based on her personality.

14. This quote and the next are from Rosa Parks, interview by E. D. (Edgar Daniel) Nixon for *America They Loved You Madly,* a precursor to *Eyes on the Prize,* February 23, 1979. Discussion centers on the Montgomery bus boycott. Film and transcript available at University Libraries online, Washington University in St. Louis, http://repository.wustl.edu/concern/videos/v405sc21t.

15. See Parks with Haskins, *Rosa Parks,* 112.

16. These biographical details are based on ibid., 3–21.

17. Ibid., 15.

18. This quote and the rest in this paragraph are from ibid., 16.

19. This quote and the rest in this paragraph are from ibid., 30–31.

20. Ibid., 56.

21. This quote and the next are from ibid., 58–59.

22. Theoharis, *Rebellious Life of Mrs. Rosa Parks,* 29.

23. Ervin Dyer, "She Recalls Civil Rights Struggles in Alabama," *Pittsburgh-Post Gazette,* February 7, 2006, B-1.

24. This description of what happened and the quotes are from Parks with Haskins, *Rosa Parks,* 115–16.

25. Ibid., 115, cites remembering her grandfather's gun.

26. Ibid., 112–13.

27. Ibid., 115–16.

28. "1,000 Hear Heroine of Alabama," *Baltimore Afro-American,* October 6, 1956, 8.

29. Parks with Haskins, *Rosa Parks,* 77.

30. This exchange is from ibid., 116.

31. This conversation is from ibid., 121.

32. This quote and the next are from ibid., 123.

33. Many people take credit for planning the boycott, and there were many contributors, but Parks and Gray put E. D. Nixon center stage (and so does Nixon). The story told here follows their outline.

34. From Parks, interview by Nixon, February 23, 1979. I edited the quote to remove duplicate words, but otherwise it is reproduced here verbatim.

35. Parks with Haskins, *Rosa Parks,* 125.

36. Ibid., 124.

37. Theoharis, *Rebellious Life of Mrs. Rosa Parks,* 76.

38. "The Ghost of Emmett Till," editorial, *New York Times* online, July 31, 2005, https://www.nytimes.com/2004/03/22/opinion/the-ghost -of-emmett-till.html?searchResultPosition=1.

39. This quote and the others in this paragraph come from Parks, interview by Nixon, February 23, 1979. I edited the quotes with ellipses, but otherwise they are verbatim.

40. This version of events is based on Gray, *Bus Ride to Justice,* 40–41. See Theoharis, *Rebellious Life of Mrs. Rosa Parks,* 80, for a slightly different description.

41. From Jo Ann Robinson, interview by Orlando Bagwell for *America They Loved You Madly,* a precursor to *Eyes on the Prize,* August 27, 1979. Film and transcript available at University Libraries online, Washington University in St. Louis, http://repository.wustl.edu /concern/videos/37720f54k.

42. This is a condensed version that appears in Parks with Haskins, *Rosa Parks,* 130.

43. The three o'clock call is mentioned in Theoharis, *Rebellious Life of Mrs. Rosa Parks,* 80.

44. The quote is from Parks, interview by Nixon, February 23, 1979.

45. Ibid.

46. See ibid. and Parks and Haskins, *Rosa Parks,* 127.

47. Jannell McGrew, "Rosa Parks' Childhood Friend, Civil Rights Leader Recalls Montgomery Bus Boycott," *Montgomery (AL) Advertiser* online, December 4, 2018, https://www.montgomeryadvertiser.com/story/news/2018/12/04/johnnie-carr-voices-montgomery-bus-boycott/2206476002.

48. Joe Azbell, "Negro Groups Ready Boycott of City Lines," *Montgomery (AL) Advertiser,* December 4, 1955, 1.

49. Ibid.

50. The quote is from Parks, interview by Nixon, February 23, 1979.

51. Al Benn, "'None of Us Knew Where It Was Going to Lead': Reporter Recalls the Early Days of the Bus Boycott," *Montgomery (AL) Advertiser* online, December 4, 2018, https://www.montgomeryadvertiser.com/story/news/2018/12/04/montgomery-bus-boycott-how-did-white-newspapers-cover-civil-rights-movement/2197482002.

52. The estimates and the quotes are from Joe Azbell, "5,000 at Meeting Outline Boycott; Bullet Clips Bus," *Montgomery Advertiser,* December 6, 1955, 1.

53. Gray, *Bus Ride to Justice,* 57.

54. Associated Press, "Buses Boycotted Over Race Issue; Montgomery, Ala., Negroes Protest Woman's Arrest for Defying Segregation," *New York Times,* December 6, 1955, 31.

55. Parks with Haskins, *Rosa Parks,* 132.

56. Parks, interview by Nixon, February 23, 1979.

57. Parks with Haskins, *Rosa Parks,* 138.

58. This quote and the next come from Martin Luther King's complete speech, which is part of "MIA Mass Meeting at Holt Street Baptist Church (December 5, 1955, Montgomery, Alabama) (transcript),

Martin Luther King Jr. Paper Project, Martin Luther King Jr. Research and Education Institute online, Stanford University, available at https://kinginstitute.stanford.edu/king-papers/documents/mia-mass-meeting-holt-street-baptist-church.

59. Ibid.

60. Parks with Haskins, *Rosa Parks,* 140.

61. This quote and the next are from Associated Press, "Peace Parley Fails in Bus Boycott," *Oakland Tribune,* December 9, 1955, E13.

62. "Boycott Still On; Bus Co. Loses $3,000 Daily," *Baltimore Afro-American,* December 17, 1955, 1.

63. "Bus Boycott Gets Tighter," *Baltimore Afro-American,* December 31, 1955, 1.

64. "Boycott Still On," 1.

65. "Alabama Bus Boycott Forces Boost in Fares," *Chicago Defender,* January 21, 1956, 4.

66. See "Jail Bus Boycott Leader," *Baltimore Afro-American,* February 4, 1956, 1.

67. Ibid.

68. Associated Press, "Blast at Negro's Home; Bomb Is Thrown in Yard of Montgomery Leader," February 2, 1956, *New York Times,* 26.

69. The quote is from "Jail Bus Boycott Leader," 1.

70. This paragraph is based on Theoharis, *Rebellious Life of Mrs. Rosa Parks,* 101.

71. Ibid.

72. This quote and the next are from Paul Hendrickson, "Montgomery; The Supporting Actors in the Historic Bus Boycott," *Washington Post,* July 24, 1989, B1.

73. "Montgomery, Ala, Bus Boycott Ends as Court Order Bars Segregation," *Washington Post,* December 21, 1956, A3.

74. Associated Press, "Negroes Will Ride Montgomery Buses in Bias Test Today," *New York Times,* December 21, 1956, 1.

75. Theoharis, *Rebellious Life of Mrs. Rosa Parks,* 82.

76. Parks with Haskins, *Rosa Parks,* 175.

77. From a speech by Martin Luther King, Monmouth College, NJ, October 6, 1966 (transcript), https://www.monmouth.edu/about/wp-content/uploads/sites/128/2019/01/MLKJrSpeechatMonmouth.pdf.

78. U.S. Federal News Service, "Sen. Reid Tribute to Rosa Parks," October 25, 2005.

CHAPTER 6   MEDICAL CRISES AND PANDEMICS

1. Katie Thomas and Denise Grady, "Trump's Embrace of a Drug Goes Against Science," *New York Times,* March 21, 2020, 13.

2. This quote and the next two are from Rita Rubin, "Unapproved Drugs Ignite Life-and-Death Debate; Lawsuit Pits Desperately Ill Against Hard Bureaucratic Realities," *USA Today,* April 2, 2007, A1.

3. Maria Cheng, "Experimental Treatments Attack Cancer: In Britain, Terminally Ill May Be Able to Try New Drugs; In U.S. All Study Designs Must Have FDA Approval," *St. Louis Post-Dispatch,* April 20, 2008, A6.

4. The information in this paragraph is based on "Pioneering Treatment: Forestville Doctor Battling Brain Cancer First to Have Focused-Ultrasound Procedure," *Press Democrat* (Santa Rosa, CA), April 10, 2014, B1.

5. Ibid.

6. Ibid.

7. See "Peter Rolf Baginsky" (obituary), *Press Democrat* (Santa Rosa, CA), November 30, 2014 available at Legacy, https://www.legacy.com/obituaries/pressdemocrat/obituary.aspx?n=peter-rolf-baginsky&pid=173321455.

8. "Pioneering Treatment," B1.

9. See "Peter Rolf Baginsky" (obituary).

10. See "FDA Approves Focused Ultrasound for Tremor-Dominant Parkinson's Disease," Focused Ultrasound Foundation online, December 19, 2018, https://fusfoundation.org/the-foundation/news-media/fda-approves-focused-ultrasound-for-tremor-dominant-parkinsons-disease.

11. This quote and the next are from the video "A Message from Alex Trebek," YouTube, 1:13, *Jeopardy!,* March 6, 2019, https://www.youtube.com/watch?v=7cInGyxCY9k.

12. See "Alex Trebek Without Pants?," YouTube, 0:43, monkeydog sushi, uploaded February 13, 2007, https://www.youtube.com/watch?v=1zWagEnd9Xs.

13. Marianne Garvey, "Alex Trebek Discusses the Latest in His Cancer Battle," CNN online, December 30, 2019, https://www.cnn.com/2019/12/30/entertainment/alex-trebek-cancer-battle-trnd/index.html.

14. These numbers are from Kiran K. Khush et al., "The International Thoracic Organ Transplant Registry of the International Society for Heart and Lung Transplantation: Thirty-fifth Adult Heart Transplantation Report—2018; Focus Theme: Multiorgan Transplantation," *Journal of Heart and Lung Transplantation* 37, no. 10 (October 1, 2018): 1157.

15. "Vanguard's Bogle Waiting for Transplant," *USA Today,* October 25, 1995, B2.

16. This quote and the next are from "Nightly Business Report," CEO Wire, Waltham, November 25, 2004.

17. The description and quotes in this paragraph are from, Erin Arvendlund, "Vanguard Founder Bogle and Surgeons Gather for a Heart-Transplant Reunion," *Philadelphia Inquirer* online, February 21, 2017, https://www.inquirer.com/philly/business/personal_finance/87-Yr-Old-Vanguard-Founder-John-Bogle-Hearts-His-Heart-Transplant.html.

18. The story in this paragraph and continued in the next is based on Steven Ginsberg, "One Life Galvanizes Thousands; Out of Options, Va. Woman Fights for Experimental Cancer Drugs," *Washington Post,* May 7, 2001, B1.

19. Ibid.

20. Ibid.

21. Ibid.

22. Steven Ginsberg, "'We've Gone from Hopeless to Hope'; U-Va. Student Battling Rare Form of Cancer Gets Into Experimental Drug Program," *Washington Post,* June 6, 2001, B3. Abigail was admitted to a program by OSI Pharmaceuticals, a small firm in Uniondale, New York, as well as a new trial at AstraZeneca.

23. Steven Ginsberg, "Student Dies After Fight with Drug Firms; Cancer Patient, 21, Sought Alternatives," *Washington Post,* June 12, 2001, B7.

24. Ginsberg, "'Hopeless to Hope,'" B3.

25. Valerie A. Palda et al., "'Futile' Care: Do We Provide It? Why? A Semistructured, Canada-Wide Survey of Intensive Care Unit Doctors and Nurses," *Journal of Critical Care* 20, no. 3 (2005): 210.

26. Ginsberg, "'Hopeless to Hope,'" B3.

27. This quote and the remaining in this paragraph are from Lindy Willmot et al., "Reasons Doctors Provide Futile Treatment at the End of Life: A Qualitative Study," *Journal of Medical Ethics* 42, no. 8 (August 2016): 496 and 499.

28. This quote and the next are from Thanh N. Huynh et al., "The Opportunity Cost of Futile Treatment in the ICU," *Critical Care Medicine* 42, no. 9 (September 2014): 1981.

29. Peter Sands et al., "The Neglected Dimension of Global Security—A Framework for Countering Infectious-Disease Crises," *New England Journal of Medicine* 374, no. 13 (March 31, 2016): 1281–87.

30. Ibid., 1281.

31. Ibid.

32. The most prominent comment came from a blog by Lawrence H. Summers, "This Is a Global Threat as Big as Climate Change," *Wonkblog* (blog), *Washington Post,* January 13, 2016, https://www .washingtonpost.com/news/wonk/wp/2016/01/13/this-is-a-global -threat-as-big-as-climate-change/.

33. This quote and the next are from Sands et al., "Neglected Dimension of Global Security," 1284.

34. Summers, "Global Threat."

35. Sands et al., "Neglected Dimension," 1284.

36. *Mitigating the Impact of Pandemic Influenza Through Vaccine Innovation* (Washington, D.C.: Council of Economic Advisers, September 2019), https://www.hsdl.org/?view&did=831583.

37. Ibid., 3.

38. Ibid.

39. Ibid., 36.

40. "Council of Economic Advisers," Employment Act of 1946, available at Council of Economic Advisers online, https://www.whitehouse .gov/cea. For a nice discussion of the Employment Act of 1946 see, "Employment Act of 1946," Federal Reserve History, November 22, 2013, https://www.federalreservehistory.org/essays/employment-act -of-1946.

41. *Mitigating the Impact of Pandemic Influenza,* 1.

42. On September 19, 2019, coincident with the release of the CEA re-port, President Donald Trump signed an executive order entitled Modernizing Influenza Vaccines in the United States to Promote National Security and Public Health, which continued vaccine work conducted by federal agencies since 2005. The executive order also established a National Influenza Vaccine Task Force and requested a report within 120 days. It asked the Task Force to outline a five-year national plan "to promote the use of more agile and scalable vaccine

manufacturing technologies and to accelerate development of vaccines that protect against many or all influenza viruses." That report was due on January 19, 2020, but a search of the public press failed to uncover it. For background, see Targeted News Service, "President Trump Issues Executive Order on Modernizing Influenza Vaccines in U.S. to Promote National Security, Public Health," September 19, 2019, and Sarah Owermohle and Sarah Karlin-Smith, "Pelosi's Plan Has Landed," Politico, September 20, 2019.

43. The quote is from Gina Kolata, *Flu: The Story of the Great Influenza Pandemic of 1918 and the Search for the Virus That Caused It* (New York: Farrar, Straus and Giroux, 1999), 143.

44. Roger W. Evans, "Health Care Technology and the Inevitability of Resource Allocation and Rationing Decisions," *Journal of the American Medical Association* (*JAMA*) 249, no. 16 (April 22/29, 1983): 2208.

45. The U.S. Department of Health and Human Services administers the Strategic National Stockpile (SNS), which is designed and resourced to address discrete events like smaller, limited displacements or localized disasters, such as hurricanes or terrorist attacks. According to *The New York Times Magazine* (November 22, 2020, 24): "In 2009, the Obama administration disbursed 85 million respirators from the S.N.S. while combating the H1N1 pandemic, and then failed to effectively replace them, despite being warned to do so. The Trump administration also did not refill the stockpile, ignoring admonitions from public health officials and a pandemic-simulation test that showed America would run disastrously short of P.P.E. if the real thing occurred."

CHAPTER 7   ROGUE TRADERS

1. Heather Long, "How We Turned $500,000 into $1.3 Million in a Month," CNN Business online, November 18, 2015, https://money.cnn.com/2015/11/18/investing/td-ameritrade-investing-competition-winners-zac-rankin/index.html.

2. Ibid.

3. See "Trader Sent to Clean Up Backroom Woes Left a Globe Rattling Mess," *Wall Street Journal,* February 28, 1995, A3, for a description of Nick Leeson.

4. Nick Leeson with Edward Whitley, *Rogue Trader: The Original Story of the Banker Who Broke the System* (London: Little Brown, 1996), 45.

5. Ibid., 28, for this quote and the next two in this paragraph.

6. Ibid., 29.

7. John Darnton, "Inside Barings, a Clash of Two Banking Eras," *New York Times,* March 6, 1995, A1.

8. For details, see Stephen Fay, *The Collapse of Barings* (New York: W. W. Norton, 1996), 10.

9. A nice discussion of the bailout is Eugene N. White, "How to Prevent a Banking Panic: The Barings Crisis of 1890" (paper presented at the Annual Meeting of the Economic History Association, Boulder, CO, September 16–18, 2016), https://www.eh.net/eha/wp-content/uploads/2016/08/White.pdf.

10. Nick Leeson claims in Leeson with Whitley, *Rogue Trader,* 50, that he did not speculate until his second year on Simex, but *The Report of the Inspectors Appointed by the Minister of Finance* (Singapore, Ministry of Finance, 1995), 20, para. 3.13 (*Singapore Report* going forward), https://eresources.nlb.gov.sg/printheritage/detail/afc97ab2-d21f-470e-a1c1-4c2de3c57854.aspx, suggests that his speculation began immediately.

11. For the 3-to-1 ratio, see *Report of the Board of Banking Supervision Inquiry into the Circumstances of the Collapse of Barings* (*Banking Report* going forward) (London: Her Majesty's Stationery Office [HMSO], July 18, 1995), 35, paras. 2.81–2.85, https://assets.publishing.service.gov.uk/government/uploads/system/uploads/attachment_data/file/235622/0673.pdf.

12. Leeson with Whitley, *Rogue Trader,* 172.

13. Ibid., 63.

14. See *Banking Report,* 44, paras. 3.35–3.39, for a discussion of Leeson's proposed arbitrage strategy.

15. See Stephen Quinn, "Gold, Silver, and the Glorious Revolution: Arbitrage Between Bills of Exchange and Bullion," *Economic History Review* 49, no. 3 (August 1996): 473–90.

16. See *Banking Report,* 199, para. 12.34.

17. Leeson with Whitley, *Rogue Trader,* 99.

18. Ibid., 108–9.

19. Cumulative losses in Leeson's hidden 88888 error account are reported monthly between July 1992 and February 1995 in appendix 3K in the *Singapore Report.* The loss as of December 1992 was 377 million yen, which translates into $3 million at an exchange rate of 125 yen per U.S. dollar and £2 million at an exchange rate of $1.5 per £1. The 1993 figure comes from a reported loss of 4,023 million yen, which translates into £24 million at end-of-year exchange rates.

20. See *Banking Report,* 8, paras. 1.42–1.48, for a brief summary of Leeson's subterfuge. Sections 5 and 6 (78–118) give the details.

21. Leeson with Whitley, *Rogue Trader,* 88.

22. For a formal analysis of Leeson's accounting scam, see Edward J. Kane and Kimberly DeTrask, "Breakdown of Accounting Controls at Barings and Daiwa: Benefits of Using Opportunity-Cost Measures for Trading Activity," *Pacific-Basin Finance Journal* 7, nos. 3/4 (August 1999): 203–28.

23. Leeson with Whitley, *Rogue Trader,* 113.

24. See *Banking Report,* 146, para. 9.21.

25. Ibid., 147.

26. The cumulative loss of 25,552 million yen in the 88888 account re-

ported in appendix 3K in the *Singapore Report* translates into £164 million at prevailing end-of-year exchange rates.

27. Leeson with Whitley, *Rogue Trader,* 109.

28. Benjamin Weiser, "Wall Street Weighs Its Own Vulnerability to Rogue Traders," *Washington Post,* February 28, 1997, C1.

29. For a formal analysis of Leeson's doubling strategy, see Stephen J. Brown and Onno W. Steenbeek, "Doubling: Nick Leeson's Trading Strategy," *Pacific Basin Finance Journal* 9, no. 2: (April 2001).

30. See *Banking Report,* 61, para. 4.2. The more than £100 million loss combines a loss of £34 million in Nikkei futures and £69 million in options.

31. For the narrative description, see ibid., 61–62, paras. 4.24–4.27. The estimated loss comes from appendix 3K in the *Singapore Report,* which records a loss at the end of February of 135,499 million yen (£886 million at prevailing exchange rates). Barings capital was £465 million based on the *Singapore Report,* 100, para. 13.23.

32. See ibid., 154, para. 17.25.

33. "Britain's Barings PLC Bets on Derivatives—And the Cost Is Dear," *Wall Street Journal,* February 27, 1995, A1.

34. Nicholas Bray, "Barings Was Warned Controls Were Lax but Didn't Make Reforms in Singapore," *Wall Street Journal,* March 2, 1995, A3.

35. *Banking Report,* 50, para. 3.65.

36. Leeson with Whitley, *Rogue Trader,* 250.

37. Saul Hansell, "For Rogue Traders, Yet Another Victim," *New York Times,* February 28, 1995, D1.

38. Barbara Sullivan and Ray Moseley, "Old Bank, Modern Scandal," *Chicago Tribune,* February 28, 1995, D1.

39. *Banking Report,* 8, para. 1.45.

40. See John Gapper and Nicholas Denton, *All That Glitters: The Fall of Barings* (London: Penguin, 1996), 330.

41. "Leeson Loses Barings," *Wall Street Journal,* February 28, 1995, A20.

42. This quote and the next are from Associated Press, "Singapore Sentences Leeson to 6½ Years in Prison," *New York Times,* December 2, 1995, A35.

43. This quote and the next are from Michael Lewis, *Liar's Poker: Rising Through the Wreckage on Wall Street* (New York: W. W. Norton, 1989), 155, 157.

44. Ibid., 157.

45. Steve Swartz, "Merrill Lynch Trader Blamed in Big Loss Had Been Under Supervision, Aides Say," *Wall Street Journal,* May 1, 1987, 6.

46. Steve Swartz, "Merrill Lynch Posts $250 Million of Mortgage-Issue Trading Losses," *Wall Street Journal,* April 30, 1987, 2.

47. Michael A. Hiltzik, "Merrill Lynch Has Bond Loss of $250 Million," *Los Angeles Times,* April 30, 1987, C1.

48. James Sterngold, "Anatomy of a Staggering Loss," *New York Times,* May 11, 1987, D1.

49. Alison Leigh Cowan, "2 Resign at Merrill," *New York Times,* May 20, 1987, D6.

50. Steve Swartz, "Bear Stearns Hires Trader Blamed by Merrill for Loss," *Wall Street Journal,* November 4, 1987, 42.

51. This quote and the next are from Michael Siconolfi, "Talented Outsiders: Bear Stearns Prospers Hiring Daring Traders That Rival Firms Shun," *Wall Street Journal,* November 11, 1993, A1.

52. Justin Bear, "Ex- Bear Stearns CEO Is Off Wall Street but Still Mixing It Up at the Bridge Table," *Wall Street Journal* (online) March 17, 2018, https://www.wsj.com/articles/ex-bear-stearns-ceo-off-wall-street-but-still-mixing-it-up-at-the-bridge-table-1521288000.

53. Matt Egan, "The Stunning Downfall of Bear Stearns and Its Bridge-Playing CEO," CNN Business online, September 30, 2018, https://www.cnn.com/2018/09/30/investing/bear-stearns-2008-crisis-jimmy-cayne/index.html.

CHAPTER 8   ADOLF HITLER AND THE BATTLE OF THE BULGE

1. See Richard Evans, "Why Did Stauffenberg Plant the Bomb?," *Süddeutsche Zeitung,* January 23, 2009, available at http://www.signandsight.com/features/1824.html, for a discussion of Stauffenberg's philosophy and his desire for a negotiated peace.

2. See Ian Kershaw, *Hitler, 1936–1945 Nemesis* (New York: W. W. Norton, 2000), 693.

3. Percy Ernst Schramm, *Hitler: The Man & the Military Leader* (Chicago: Academy Chicago Publishers, 1981), 163.

4. This quote and the next are from "Eisenhower to His Troops: 'Defeat Nazi Final Gamble,'" *Christian Science Monitor,* December 22, 1944, 1.

5. A transcript of this meeting appears in Gerhard L. Weinberg, Helmut Heiber, and David M. Glantz, *Hitler and His Generals: Military Conferences 1942–1945* (New York: Enigma Books, 2003), 444–63.

6. Ibid., 446–47 and 450 for the quotes in this paragraph.

7. This incident and the quotes that follow are from Seymour Freiden and William Richardson, eds., *The Fatal Decisions* (New York: Berkley, 1956), 203–4.

8. Ibid., 206.

9. Schramm, *Hitler,* 168.

10. The quotes in this paragraph are from a transcript of a meeting on August 31, 1944, in Weinberg, Heiber, and Glantz, *Hitler and His Generals,* 466–67.

11. Schramm, *Hitler,* 176.

12. I have reconstructed this meeting from a number of sources: (1) Werner Kreipe, *The Personal Diary of Gen. Fl. Kreipe, Chief of the Luftwaffe General Staff During the Period 22 July–2 November 1944* (n.p., 1947); (2) Charles V. P. von Luttichau, "The German Counteroffensive in the Ardennes," chap. 20 in *Command Decisions* (Washington, D.C.:

Center of Military History, U.S. Army, 1960); (3) Hugh M. Cole, *The Ardennes, Battle of the Bulge* (Washington, D.C.: Center of Military History, US Army, 1993; (4) Peter Caddick-Adams, *Snow and Steel: The Battle of the Bulge, 1944–1945* (New York: Oxford University Press, 2015).

13. Kreipe, *Personal Diary,* 24, reads as follows: "Fuhrer interrupts Jodl. Decision by the Fuhrer, counterattack from the Ardennes, objective Antwerp." I use the quote from Cole, *Ardennes,* 2, which may reflect other sources.

14. Kreipe, *Personal Diary,* 24.

15. See Jacques Nobecourt, *Hitler's Last Gamble: The Battle of the Bulge,* trans. R. H. Barry (New York: Belmont Tower Books, 1967), 39. The quote is from Hitler's *Mein Kampf.*

16. Weinberg, Heiber, and Glantz, *Hitler and His Generals,* 540.

17. Kreipe, *Personal Diary,* 24.

18. See "To the Rhine," *New York Times,* November 26, 1944, E1; "Americans Advance on Rhine 'Gateways,'" *Irish Times,* November 28, 1944, 1; and "Two Novembers: Germany's Position in 1918 and 1944," *Manchester (UK) Guardian,* November 13, 1944, 4.

19. "Two Novembers," 4.

20. Freiden and Richardson, *Fatal Decisions,* 231.

21. This quote and the next are from ibid., 236.

22. Cole, *Ardennes,* 69.

23. This quote and the next are from Freiden and Richardson, *Fatal Decisions,* 233–34.

24. This story comes from Harry C. Butcher, *My Three Years with Eisenhower: The Personal Diary of Captain Harry C. Butcher, USNR, Naval Aide to General Eisenhower, 1942–1945* (New York: Simon & Schuster, 1946), 722.

25. Caddick-Adams, *Snow and Steel,* 265.

26. Ibid.

27. This quote and the next are from Dwight D. Eisenhower, "Eisenhower Vowed Never to Let the Enemy's Bulge Cross the Meuse," *Washington Post,* November 26, 1948, 1.

28. This quote and the next are from Freiden and Richardson, *Fatal Decisions,* 262.

29. Nobecourt, *Hitler's Last Gamble,* 279.

30. "Stimson Says Nazis Losing Great Gamble," *Hartford Courant,* December 29, 1944, 1.

31. See Caddick-Adams, *Snow and Steel,* 348–49.

32. The description of this incident is based on a number of sources, including Trevor N. Dupuy, *Hitler's Last Gamble: The Battle of the Bulge, December 1944–January 1945* (New York: HarperCollins, 1994), 64–65 and appendix G; Caddick-Adams, *Snow and Steel,* 559–77; and Cole, *Ardennes,* 260ff.

33. This quote and the next come from "Malmédy Survivor Recalls Massacre," U.S. Fed News Service, Washington, D.C., December 21, 2007.

34. See Hal Boyle, "Yanks Dig in at Scene of Buddies' Massacre," *Los Angeles Times,* January 15, 1945, 5.

35. A summary of the trial appears in Fred L. Borch III, "The 'Malmedy Massacre' Trial: The Military Government Court Proceedings and the Controversial Legal Aftermath," *The Army Lawyer,* special issue, *Lore of the Corps,* March 2012, 22–27. A video recording of trial excerpts is available at "Malmedy Massacre Trial Uncut," YouTube, 53.12, Lumiere Media, October 2, 2011, https://www.youtube.com/watch?v=u5X0VyAJUOo.

36. United Press, "Laughing Germans Slew Captives, 'Bulge' Massacre Survivors Say," *New York Times,* May 22, 1946, 4.

37. See Caddick-Adams, *Snow and Steel,* 572, which identifies the man as George Fleps. But see United Press, "Laughing Germans Slew Captives," 4, which identifies the man as George Fletz.

38. "Massacre of Yanks Ordered, Panzer Officer Tells Court," *Washington Post,* May 21, 1946, 2.

39. Associated Press, "SS Troops Confirm Massacre Orders," *New York Times,* May 19, 1946, 25.

40. See "Malmedy Massacre Trial Uncut," Lumiere Media.

41. United Press, "SS Blames Hitler in Bulge Murders," *New York Times,* May 18, 1946, 6.

42. Ibid.

43. Nobecourt, *Hitler's Last Gamble,* 121.

44. Dupuy, *Hitler's Last Gamble,* 5.

45. Caddick-Adams, *Snow and Steel,* 253.

46. Borch, "'Malmedy Massacre' Trial," 26.

47. These details are from Robert Daley, "The Case of the SS Hero," *The New York Times Magazine,* November 7, 1976, 32.

48. Paul Webster, "Ex-SS Man Killed by Avengers," *Guardian* (UK edition), July 16, 1976, 2.

49. See Weinberg, Heiber, and Glantz, *Hitler and His Generals,* 468.

50. Thomas Fleming, "A Policy Written in Blood," *Quarterly Journal of Military History* 21, no. 2 (Winter 2009): 28.

51. Associated Press, "Peace Must Let Germans Live, Says Goebbels," *Chicago Daily Tribune,* October 28, 1944, 5.

52. Philip M. Taylor and N. C. F. Weekes, "Breaking the German Will to Resist, 1944–1945: Allied Efforts to End World War II by Nonmilitary Means," *Historical Journal of Film, Radio and Television* 18, no. 1 (March 1998): 7–8.

53. See Butcher, *My Three Years with Eisenhower,* 518.

CHAPTER 9   PRISON VIOLENCE

1. Gary Marx and Tracy Dell'Angela, "2 Paths for Prison Lifers: Wither Away or Adjust," *Chicago Tribune,* January 21, 1996, 1.

2. This quote and the next are from Judy Tatham, "Judge: Gruesome Murder Deserves Life," *Herald & Review* (Decatur, IL), September 8, 1990, 3. This article gives March 25, 1990, as the date of the murder and is the last in a series published in the *Herald & Review* that began in July 1990. The details of the planning and the attack described in this paragraph come from those articles.

3. Steven A. Holmes, "Inmate Violence Is on Rise as Federal Prisons Change," *New York Times,* February 9, 1995, A1.

4. The information in this paragraph is based on Alan Abrahamson and Phil Sneiderman, "Inmates Strike over Bid to Curb Conjugal Visits," *Los Angeles Times,* March 1, 1995, 1.

5. Mike Ward, "Behind Bars, 'Predators' Thrive; Board Today Will Examine the Growing Violence in Texas Prisons Such as the Death of Randy Payne," *Austin American-Statesman,* November 17, 1994, A1.

6. "No Escape: Male Rape in U.S. Prisons," *Human Rights Watch Report* (April 2001): 11–12.

7. Ibid., 13.

8. Ibid.

9. Ibid., 14.

10. Ward, "Behind Bars, 'Predators' Thrive," A1.

11. The data and information in this paragraph come from "Fact Sheet: Trends in U.S. Corrections—U.S. State and Federal Prison Population, 1925–2017," the Sentencing Project online, June 2019, https://www.sentencingproject.org/wp-content/uploads/2016/01/Trends-in-US-Corrections.pdf.

12. This discussion and the associated quotes come from three articles in the *Chicago Tribune:* "Guilty Plea in Shooting Death," August 24, 1993, sec. 3, 3; Gary Marx, "Prison Pairing Leads to Slaying," June 9, 2009, 1; and Steve Schmadeke, "Inmate Sentenced in Killing That Changed How Prison System Houses Nonviolent Offenders," January 18, 2012, https://www.chicagotribune.com/news/ct-xpm

-2012-01-18-ct-met-inmate-sentenced-0119-20120119-story
.html.

13. The information and quotes in this paragraph and the next two (except where noted) come from the following articles: Gary Marx, "Prison Experts See Fatal Mistake," *Chicago Tribune,* May 5, 2009, 5; Nicholas J. C. Pistor, "Illinois Reaches Settlement in Menard Suit. Family of Murdered Inmate Alleged Correction Officers Knew He Was in Danger," *St. Louis Post-Dispatch,* January 6, 2009, B3; and "Slain Inmate's Family Awarded $13 Million," *Daily Herald* (Arlington Heights, IL), January 6, 2009, 3.

14. This quote is from Christie Thompson and Joe Shapiro, "The Deadly Consequences of Solitary with a Cellmate," the Marshall Project online, March 24, 2016, https://www.themarshallproject.org/2016/03/24/the-deadly-consequences-of-solitary-with-a-cellmate.

15. Marx, "Prison Experts See Fatal Mistake," 5.

16. Much of the biographical information below comes from Silverstein's obituary: Sam Roberts, "Thomas Silverstein, Killer and Most Isolated Inmate, Dies at 67," *New York Times* online, May 21, 2019, https://www.nytimes.com/2019/05/21/obituaries/thomas-silverstein-dead.html?searchResultPosition=1.

17. Michael Satchell, "The End of the Line: It's Known Among Its Inhabitants as the Toughest Prison in America. The New Alcatraz. Marion, Illinois," *Parade,* September 28, 1980, 4.

18. Ibid.

19. The dates November 22, 1981, and September 27, 1982, (below) come from the account of the murders described in Pete Early, *The Hot House* (New York: Bantam Books, 1992), 194–207.

20. Ibid., 202ff.

21. Lynn Emmerman, "2 Racists Suspected in Prison Deaths," *Chicago Tribune,* October 30, 1983, A1.

22. "Life Sentence in Sniper Shootings," *Philadelphia Inquirer,* October 5, 1991, B5.

23. This quote and the next are from James A. Paluch Jr., *A Life for a Life* (Los Angeles: Roxbury, 2004), 175–76.

24. Marx and Dell'Angela, "2 Paths for Prison Lifers, 1.

25. "Life Without Parole: Hope Springs Eternal," *Los Angeles Times,* June 14, 1988, 4.

26. Early, *The Hot House,* 87.

27. This quote is from Marx and Dell'Angela, "2 Paths for Prison Lifers," 1.

28. Ibid.

29. This quote and the next are from Patrik Jonsson, "One Warden's Way of Instilling Hope Behind Bars," *Christian Science Monitor,* November 14, 2007, 1.

30. Margaret E. Leigey, *The Forgotten Men: Serving a Life Without Parole Sentence* (New Brunswick, NJ: Rutgers University Press, 2015), 52.

31. Mark D. Cunningham and Jon R. Sorensen, "Nothing to Lose? A Comparative Examination of Prison Misconduct Rates Among Life Without Parole and Other Long-term Security Inmates," *Criminal Justice and Behavior* 33, no. 6 (December 2006): 683–705.

32. Ibid., 694 and 699.

33. Timothy J. Flanigan, "Time Served and Institutional Misconduct: Patterns of Involvement in Disciplinary Infractions Among Long-term and Short-term Inmates," *Journal of Criminal Justice* 8 (1980): 364.

34. Robert Johnson and Sandra McGunigall-Smith, "Life Without Parole, America's Other Death Penalty," *Prison Journal* 88, no. 2 (June 2008): 331.

35. Paluch, *A Life for a Life,* 98.

36. The information and quotes in this paragraph are from Allison Gatlin, "Soledad Lifers Advise Short-Timers in Prison Program," *Salinas (CA) Weekend Californian,* June 1, 2013, 1A.

37. See Marx and Dell'Angela, "2 Paths for Prison Lifers," 1.

38. The previous quotes and the story are from "Restricted Access Inmates Maintain Course," *Boston Globe,* May 17, 2005, D1.

39. This quote and the remaining quotes in the paragraph are from Shaila K. Dewan, "Golf Course Shaped by Prisoner Hands," *New York Times* online, August 15, 2004, https://www.nytimes.com/2004/08/15/us/golf -course-shaped-by-prisoners-hands.html?searchResultPosition=1.

40. The quotes and the story come from Lou Carlozo, "Prison Blues," *Chicago Tribune,* February 18, 2002, sec. 5, 1.

CHAPTER 10   MOHAMED ATTA AND SUICIDE TERRORISTS

1. The details and quotes in this and the next three paragraphs come from Uli Schmetzer, "Italian Hostage Siege at Impasse," *Chicago Tribune,* August 27, 1987, 8, and United Press International, "Six Prisoners End Elba Siege, Free Hostages," *Los Angeles Times,* September 2, 1987, 2.

2. These numbers and the definition of mass shootings discussed in this paragraph are based on "The Mother Jones Mass Shootings Data Base, 1982–2019," *Mother Jones* online, https://www.motherjones .com/politics/2012/12/mass-shootings-mother-jones-full-data/. I adjusted the numbers to keep the definition of murders at four, so they are consistent both pre- and post-2001. The definition was lowered to three or more deaths in 2012 by the Obama administration.

3. I calculated the post-2001 number on the four-person definition of mass shootings, so that it is comparable to the pre-2001 period. There was no trend in the pre-2001 numbers to suggest a gradual uptrend in mass shootings rather than a discrete jump after 2001. In particular, breaking the pre-2001 period into three periods of six years each produced an annual average number of mass murders in the three periods of one, two, and two. By way of contrast, the three six-year intervals after 2001 have annual average incidents of two, four, and four.

4. The information in this paragraph is based on Robert A. Pape, *Dying to Win: The Strategic Logic of Suicide Terrorism* (New York: Random House Trade Paperbacks, 2005), 12–13.

5. The information in this paragraph is based on Iain Overton, "A Short History of Suicide Bombing," Action on Armed Violence (AOAV) online, August 23, 2019, https://aoav.org.uk/2013/a-short-history -of-suicide-bombings.

6. Pape, *Dying to Win,* 12.

7. Bernard Lewis, *The Crisis of Islam: Holy War and Unholy Terrorism* (New York: Random House, 2003), 144.

8. Based on Pape, *Dying to Win,* 4.

9. This quote and the next are from "Last Words of a Terrorist," *Guardian* (U.S. edition) online, September 30, 2001, https://www .theguardian.com/world/2001/sep/30/terrorism.september113.

10. Much of the biographical information in this and the next paragraph is from Terry McDermott, "A Perfect Soldier: Mohamed Atta, Whose Hard Gaze Has Stared from a Billion Television Screens and Newspaper Pages, Has Become, for Many, the Face of Evil Incarnate," *Los Angeles Times,* January 27, 2002, A1.

11. This quote and the next are from Neil MacFarquhar, Jim Yardley, and Paul Zielbauer, "A Portrait of the Terrorist: From Shy Child to Single-Minded Killer," *New York Times,* October 10, 2001, B9.

12. *The 9/11 Commission Report: Final Report of the National Commission on Terrorist Attacks on the United States* (Washington, D.C.: U.S. Government Printing Office, 2004), 164, https://www.9-11commission .gov/report/911Report.pdf, blames Zammar with radicalizing Atta and the other bombers in Hamburg.

13. Terry McDermott, *Perfect Soldiers: The Hijackers—Who They Were, Why They Did It* (New York: HarperCollins, 2005), 22.

14. This quote, the next, and the information in this paragraph are from Dirk Laabs and Terry McDermott, "Prelude to 9/11: A Hijacker's

Love, Lies—Aysel Senguen Saw Her Fiance Fall into Radical Islam. She Knew Something Was Wrong but Had No Idea What Lay Ahead," *Los Angeles Times,* January 27, 2003, A1, Orange County ed.

15. McDermott, *Perfect Soldiers*, 197.

16. See *The 9/11 Commission Report,* 166.

17. Pape, *Dying to Win,* 223.

18. Denis MacEoin, "Suicide Bombing as Worship: Dimensions of Jihad," *Middle East Quarterly* 16, no. 4 (Fall 2009): 18.

19. This quote and the others in this paragraph are from Nasra Hassan, "An Arsenal of Believers: Talking to the 'Human Bombs,'" *The New Yorker,* November 19, 2001, 36–41.

20. Ibid.

21. Rebecca Leung, "Mind of the Suicide Bomber," *60 Minutes,* aired May 23, 2003, on CBS, https://www.cbsnews.com/news/mind-of -the-suicide-bomber.

22. See Pape, *Dying to Win,* 4.

23. Bernard Weinraub, "India Holds Dozens in Ghandi Killing," *New York Times,* July 14, 1991, A3.

24. John F. Burns, "4 Years After the Killing of Rajiv Gandhi, Doubts Persist," *New York Times,* September 12, 1995, A6.

25. Weinraub, "India Holds Dozens in Ghandi Killing," A3.

26. Hala Jaber, "The Avengers," *Sunday Times* (London), December 7, 2003, Features, 1, as quoted in Debra Zedalis, "Female Suicide Bombers" (research paper, U.S. Army War College, Carlisle, PA, June 2004), https://apps.dtic.mil/sti/pdfs/ADA424180.pdf.

27. See Pape, *Dying to Win,* 228, for the estimate.

28. This quote and the next are from Kate Fillion, "In Conversation with Mia Bloom: On the Rise in Female Suicide Bombings, How Women Cause More Damage and Why They Do It," *Maclean's,* Janu-

ary 24, 2011, https://www.macleans.ca/general/macleans-interview-mia-bloom/.

29. Patricia Pearson, "Hard to Imagine Female Bad Guy? Think Again," *USA Today,* January 30, 2002, A13.

30. This quote and then next are from Jan Goodwin, "When the Suicide Bomber Is a Woman," *Marie Claire* online, January 16, 2008, https://www.marieclaire.com/politics/news/a717/female-suicide-bomber/.

31. This quote and the remaining in this paragraph are from Somini Sengupta, "Sri Lanka Rejects Call for Truce, Saying Defeat of Rebels Is Near," *New York Times* online, February 6, 2009, https://www.nytimes.com/2009/02/06/world/asia/06lanka.html?searchResultPosition=1.

32. See Lydia Polgreen, "Tamils Now Languish in Sri Lanka Camps," *New York Times* online, July 12, 2009, https://www.nytimes.com/2009/07/13/world/asia/13lanka.html?searchResultPosition=1.

33. This quote and the next one are from Mark Magnier, "Looking to Sri Lanka for Lessons: The Tactics It Used to Defeat Tamil Tiger Rebels Could Help Other Nations Grappling with Insurgencies," *Los Angeles Times,* May 23, 2009, A28.

34. See Alan Dershowitz, *Why Terrorism Works: Understanding the Threat, Responding to the Challenge* (New Haven, CT: Yale University Press, 2002), 172–73.

35. Rebecca Leung, "Mind of the Suicide Bomber."

36. For evidence that home demolition reduces suicide bombings at least for a while, see Efraim Benmelech, Claude Berrebi, and Esteben Klor, "Counter-Suicide-Terrorism: Evidence from House Demolitions," *Journal of Politics* 77, no. 1 (January 2015): 27–43.

37. Ibid., 29. for a brief history of home demolition. See also Naomi Zeveloff, "Israel Is Again Demolishing Homes of Terror Suspects," *Forward,* September 12, 2014, 1.

CHAPTER 11 FREEDOM TO SUCCEED

1. The song is "Me and Bobby McGee," released posthumously in 1971 as part of the album *Pearl* after Joplin died of an accidental heroin overdose at the age of twenty-seven in October 1970. I thank my friend Alan Schoffman for bringing this to my attention.

2. Chuck Landon, "Marshall Had Nothing to Lose Against; Herd Wins Coin Toss and Doesn't Defer Kickoff for First Time All Season," *Charleston (WV) Daily Mail,* November 12, 2007, 1B.

3. Ibid.

4. This article and the quotes in this paragraph are from Milo F. Bryant, "Broncos, Wake Up and Smell the Mediocrity," *Gazette* (Colorado Springs, CO), November 24, 2003.

5. This quote and some of the biographical details are from Harry Gordon, "How the Daughter of an Ancient Race Made It Out of the Australian Outback by Hitting a Tennis Ball Sweetly and Hard," *The New York Times Magazine,* August 29, 1971, 10.

6. This quote and the next are from United Press International, "Goolagong Upsets Billie Jean, Plays Court for Wimbledon Title," *Los Angeles Times,* July 1, 1971, D1.

7. Barry Lorge, "Aussie Princess Is Back," *Washington Post,* July 4, 1979, D1.

8. The quotes are from Marian Christy, "Alan Dershowitz for the Defense; Once Harvard Law's Youngest Professor, Alan Dershowitz Loves to Fight People in Power," *Boston Globe,* January 27, 1985, A15.

9. This quote and the next are from John Herbers, "The 37th President; In Three Decades, Nixon Tasted Crisis and Defeat, Victory, Ruin, and Revival," *New York Times,* April 24, 1994, A29.

10. Christy, "Alan Dershowitz for the Defense," A15.

11. Herbers, "The 37th President," A29.

12. This quote and the remaining in this paragraph are from "Here's the History of the NFL's 'Hail Mary' Pass on Its 41st Anniversary,"

Eyewitness News, WABC-TV online, December 28, 2016, https://abc7ny.com/hail-mary-football-pass-doug-flutie/1138071.

13. For some estimates of the probabilities, which vary based on where the throw starts, see Brian Burke, "Hail Mary Probabilities," Advanced Football Analytics, September 25, 2012, http://archive.advanced footballanalytics.com/2012/09/hail-mary-probabilities.html.

14. For these numbers see "Hail Marys—Just How Improbable Are They?," September 10, 2015, https://blog.cougarstats.com/2015/09/10/hail-marys-just-how-improbable-are-they.

15. This quote and the next are from Chris Kelly, "McCain's Hail Mary Pass: Choice of Palin a Desperate Heave Doomed to Fail," *Scranton (PA) Times-Tribune,* September 7, 2008, D1.

16. Ellen Goodman, "Back to the Future," *South Florida Sun-Sentinel,* July 10, 2004, 13A.

17. See Michael Tackett, "Assets: Passion for Ideas, Appeal to Minorities," *Chicago Tribune,* August 10, 1996, 1.

18. Tim Morrison, "A History of Vice Presidential Picks, from the Pages of *Time*: Jack Kemp, 1996," *Time* online, August 10, 2012, https://newsfeed.time.com/2012/08/11/a-history-of-vice-presidential-picks-from-the-pages-of-time/slide/1996-jack-kemp.

19. This quote and the next are from Robin Finn, "Defying Her Sport's Logic, A Tennis Prodigy Emerges," *New York Times,* September 7, 1997, 1.

20. The quotes in this paragraph are from Bill Dwyre, "Venus Is Giving It Her All on Court," *Los Angeles Times,* June 24, 2014, C1.

SELECTED READINGS

CHAPTER 1 DOWNSIDE PROTECTION

Barrat, John. "Don't Pick a Fight with a Eunuch Spider. It Has Nothing to Lose." Animals, Research News, Science & Nature. Smithsonian Insider, April 7, 2011. https://insider.si.edu/2011/04/dont-pick-a-fight-with-a-eunuch-spider-its-got-nothing-to-lose/.

Black, Fischer, and Myron Scholes. "The Pricing of Options and Corporate Liabilities." *Journal of Political Economy* 81, no. 3 (May/June 1973).

Cao, Larry. "Nobel Laureate Myron Scholes on the Black-Scholes Option Pricing Model." Enterprising Investor, October 13, 2014. https://blogs.cfainstitute.org/investor/2014/10/13/nobel-laureate-myron-scholes-on-the-black-scholes-option-pricing-model.

Fitzpatrick, John C., ed. *The Writings of George Washington from the Original Manuscript Sources, 1745–1799.* Vol. 4, *October 1775–April 1776.* Washington, D.C.: Government Printing Office, 1932.

Gray, Philip, and Stephen Gray. "Testing Market Efficiency: Evidence from the NFL Sports Betting Market." *Journal of Finance* 52, no. 4 (September 1997).

"Hail Marys—Just How Improbable Are They?" CougarStats, September 10, 2015. https://blog.cougarstats.com/2015/09/10/hail-marys-just-how-improbable-are-they.

Kralj-Fiser, Simona, Matjaz Gregoric, Shichang Zhang, Daiqin Li, and Matjaz Kuntner. "Eunuchs Are Better Fighters." *Animal Behavior* 81 (2011).

Levitt, Steven. "Why Are Gambling Markets Organized So Differently from Financial Markets?" *Economic Journal* 114, no. 495 (April 2004).

Von Luttichau, Charles V. P. "The German Counteroffensive in the Ardennes." Chap. 20 in *Command Decisions,* ed. Kent Roberts Greenfield. Washington, D.C.: Center of Military History, U.S. Army, 2000. Available at Hathi Trust Digital Library, https://catalog .hathitrust.org/Record/011414502.

Trump, Donald, with Tony Schwartz. *The Art of the Deal.* New York: Ballantine Books Trade Paperback, 2015.

CHAPTER 2   LAME-DUCK U.S. PRESIDENTS

Carson, Jamie L., and Benjamin A. Kleinerman. "A Switch in Time Saves Nine: Institutions, Strategic Actors, and FDR's Court-Packing Plan." *Public Choice* 113, nos. 3 and 4 (December 2002).

Frey, Bruno S., David A. Savage, and Benno Torgler. "Behavior Under Extreme Conditions: The Titanic Disaster." *Journal of Economic Perspectives* 25, no. 1 (Winter 2011).

House, Edward Mandell. *The Intimate Papers of Colonel House: From Neutrality to War, 1915–1917.* 2 vols. Edited by Charles Seymour. Boston: Houghton Mifflin, 1926.

Ickes, Harold. *The Secret Diary of Harold L. Ickes: The First Thousand Days, 1933–1936.* New York: Simon & Schuster, 1953.

Larson, Erik. *Dead Wake.* New York: Crown, 2015.

McAdoo, William G. *Crowded Years.* Boston: Houghton Mifflin, 1931.

Neu, Charles E. *Colonel House: A Biography of Woodrow Wilson's Silent Partner.* New York: Oxford University Press, 2014.

Peifer, Douglas C. *Choosing War: Presidential Decisions in the* Maine, Lusitania, *and* Panay *Incidents.* New York: Oxford University Press, 2016.

Shlaes, Amity. *Coolidge*. New York: HarperCollins, 2013.

Shogan, Colleen. "The Contemporary Presidency: The Sixth Year Curse," *Presidential Studies Quarterly* 36, no. 1 (March 2006).

CHAPTER 3   PARDON ME

Alschuler, Albert W. "Bill Clinton's Parting Pardon Party." *Journal of Criminal Law and Criminology* 100, no. 3 (Summer 2010).

Argys, Laura, and Naci Mocan. "Who Shall Live and Who Shall Die: An Analysis of Prisoners on Death Row in the United States." *Journal of Legal Studies* 33, no. 2 (June 2004).

Duker, William F. "The President's Power to Pardon." *William and Mary Law Review* 18, no. 3 (Spring 1977).

Fowler, Kristen H. "Limiting the Federal Pardon Power." *Indiana Law Journal* 83, no. 4 (Fall 2008).

Larkin, Paul J., Jr. "The Demise of Capital Clemency." *Washington & Lee Law Review* 73, no. 3 (Summer 2016).

Love, Margaret Colgate. "The Pardon Paradox: Lessons of Clinton's Last Pardons." *Capital University Law Review* 32, no. 1 (2002).

Sisk, Gregory. "Suspending the Pardon Power During the Twilight of a Presidential Term." *Missouri Law Review* 67, no. 1 (Winter 2002).

CHAPTER 4   ASYLUM SEEKERS

Abramitzky, Ran, and Leah Boustan. "Immigration in American Economic History." *Journal of Economic Literature* 55, no. 4 (December 2017).

Allerfeldt, Kristofer. "'And We Got Here First': Albert Johnson, National Origins and Self-Interest in the Immigration Debate of the 1920s." *Journal of Contemporary History* 45, no. 1 (January 2010).

Fassin, Didier, and Estelle d'Halluin. "The Truth from the Body:

Medical Certificates as Ultimate Evidence for Asylum Seekers." *American Anthropologist* 107, no. 4 (December 2005).

Khosravi, Shahram. "Sweden: Detention and Deportation of Asylum Seekers." *Race & Class* 50, no. 4 (April 2009).

McShane, Ian. "Voyage of the Damned: MV St. Louis." *Sea Classics* 45, no. 1 (January 2012).

Robinson, Ronda. "Survivor of the Voyage of the Damned." Aish Hatorah Holocaust Studies, October 8, 2015. https://www.aish.com /ho/p/Survivor-of-the-Voyage-of-the-Damned.html.

Traub, James. "The Death of the Most Generous Nation on Earth." *Foreign Policy,* February 20, 2016.

CHAPTER 5   ROSA PARKS

Gray, Fred. *Bus Ride to Justice: Changing the System by the System.* Montgomery, AL: New South Books, 1995.

King, Martin Luther, Jr. "MIA Mass Meeting at Holt Street Baptist Church (December 5, 1955, Montgomery, Alabama) (transcript). Martin Luther King Jr. Paper Project. Martin Luther King Jr. Research and Education Institute online. Stanford University, at https:// kinginstitute.stanford.edu/king-papers/documents/mia-mass -meeting-holt-street-baptist-church.

Parks, Rosa. Interview by E. D. (Edgar Daniel) Nixon for *America They Loved You Madly*, a precursor to *Eyes on the Prize,* February 23, 1979. Discussion centers on the Montgomery bus boycott. Film and transcript available at University Libraries online, Washington University in St. Louis, http://repository.wustl.edu/concern/videos /v405sc21t.

Parks, Rosa, with Jim Haskins. *Rosa Parks: My Story.* New York: Puffin Books, 1999.

Theoharis, Jeanne. *The Rebellious Life of Mrs. Rosa Parks.* Boston: Beacon Press, 2013.

CHAPTER 6 MEDICAL CRISES AND PANDEMICS

Evans, Roger W. "Health Care Technology and the Inevitability of Resource Allocation and Rationing Decisions." *Journal of the American Medical Association (JAMA)* 249, no. 16 (April 22/29, 1983).

Huynh, Thanh N., Eric C. Kleerup, Price P. Raj, and Neil S. Wenger. "The Opportunity Cost of Futile Treatment in the ICU." *Critical Care Medicine* 42, no. 9 (September 2014).

Kolata, Gina. *Flu: The Story of the Great Influenza Pandemic of 1918 and the Search for the Virus That Caused It.* New York: Farrar, Straus and Giroux, 1999.

Mitigating the Impact of Pandemic Influenza Through Vaccine Innovation. Washington, D.C.: Council of Economic Advisers. September 2019. https://www.whitehouse.gov/wp-content/uploads/2019/09/Mitigating-the-Impact-of-Pandemic-Influenza-through-Vaccine-Innovation.pdf.

Palda, Valerie A., Kerry W. Bowman, Richard F. McLean, and Martin G. Chapman. "'Futile' Care: Do We Provide It? Why? A Semistructured, Canada-wide Survey of Intensive Care Unit Doctors and Nurses." *Journal of Critical Care* 20, no. 3 (September 2005).

Sands, Peter, Carmen Mundaca-Shah, and Victor J. Dzau. "The Neglected Dimension of Global Security—A Framework for Countering Infectious-Disease Crises." *New England Journal of Medicine* 374, no. 13 (March 31, 2016).

Willmot, Lindy, Benjamin White, Cindy Gallois, Malcolm Parker, Nicholas Graves, Sarah Winch, Leonie Kaye Callaway, Nicole Shepherd, and Eliana Close. "Reasons Doctors Provide Futile Treatment at the End of Life: A Qualitative Study." *Journal of Medical Ethics* 42, no. 8 (August 2016).

CHAPTER 7 ROGUE TRADERS

Brown, Stephen J., and Onno W. Steenbeek. "Doubling: Nick Leeson's Trading Strategy." *Pacific Basin Finance Journal* 9, no. 2 (April 2001).

Fay, Stephen. *The Collapse of Barings*. New York: W. W. Norton, 1996.

Gapper, John, and Nicholas Denton. *All That Glitters: The Fall of Barings*. London: Penguin Books, 1996.

Kane, Edward J., and Kimberly DeTrask. "Breakdown of Accounting Controls at Barings and Daiwa: Benefits of Using Opportunity-Cost Measures for Trading Activity." *Pacific-Basin Finance Journal* 7, nos. 3/4 (August 1999).

Leeson, Nick, with Edward Whitley. *Rogue Trader: The Original Story of the Banker Who Broke the System*. London: Little Brown, 1996.

Lewis, Michael, *Liar's Poker: Rising Through the Wreckage on Wall Street*. New York: W. W. Norton, 1989.

Quinn, Stephen. "Gold, Silver, and the Glorious Revolution: Arbitrage Between Bills of Exchange and Bullion." *Economic History Review* 49, no. 3 (August 1996).

White, Eugene N. "How to Prevent a Banking Panic: The Barings Crisis of 1890." Paper presented at the Annual Meeting of the Economic History Association, Boulder, CO, September 16–18, 2016, https://www.eh.net/eha/wp-content/uploads/2016/08/White.pdf.

CHAPTER 8 ADOLF HITLER AND THE BATTLE OF THE BULGE

Borch, Fred L., III. "The 'Malmédy Massacre' Trial: The Military Government Court Proceedings and the Controversial Legal Aftermath." *The Army Lawyer*, special issue, *Lore of the Corps*, March 2012.

Butcher, Harry C. *My Three Years with Eisenhower: The Personal Diary of Captain Harry C. Butcher, USNR, Naval Aide to General Eisenhower, 1942–1945*. New York: Simon & Schuster, 1946.

Caddick-Adams, Peter. *Snow and Steel: The Battle of the Bulge, 1944–1945*. New York: Oxford University Press, 2015.

Cole, Hugh M. *The Ardennes, Battle of the Bulge*. Washington, D.C.: Center of Military History, U.S. Army, 1993.

Dupuy, Trevor N. *Hitler's Last Gamble: The Battle of the Bulge, December 1944–January 1945.* New York: HarperCollins, 1994.

Fleming, Thomas. "A Policy Written in Blood." *Quarterly Journal of Military History* 21, no. 2 (Winter 2009).

Freiden, Seymour, and William Richardson, eds. *The Fatal Decisions.* New York: Berkley, 1956

Kershaw, Ian. *Hitler, 1936–1945 Nemesis.* New York: W. W. Norton, 2000.

Von Luttichau, Charles V. P. "The German Counteroffensive in the Ardennes." Chap. 20 in *Command Decisions,* ed. Kent Roberts Greenfield. Washington, D.C.: Center of Military History, U.S. Army, 2000. Available at Hathi Trust Digital Library, https://catalog .hathitrust.org/Record/011414502.

Nobecourt, Jacques. *Hitler's Last Gamble: The Battle of the Bulge.* Translated from the French by R. H. Barry. New York: Belmont Tower Books, 1967.

Schramm, Percy Ernst. *Hitler: The Man & the Military Leader.* Chicago: Academy Chicago, 1981.

Weinberg, Gerhard L., Helmut Heiber, and David M. Glantz, *Hitler and His Generals: Military Conferences 1942–1945.* New York: Enigma Books, 2003.

CHAPTER 9   PRISON VIOLENCE

Cunningham, Mark D., and Jon R. Sorensen. "Nothing to Lose? A Comparative Examination of Prison Misconduct Rates Among Life Without Parole and Other Long-term Security Inmates." *Criminal Justice and Behavior* 33, no. 6 (December 2006).

Early, Pete. *The Hot House.* New York: Bantam Books, 1992.

Flanigan, Timothy J. "Time Served and Institutional Misconduct: Patterns of Involvement in Disciplinary Infractions Among Long-term and Short-term Inmates." *Journal of Criminal Justice* 8 (1980).

Johnson, Robert, and Sandra McGunigall-Smith. "Life Without Parole, America's Other Death Penalty." *Prison Journal* 88, no. 2 (June 2008).

Leigey, Margaret E. *The Forgotten Men: Serving a Life Without Parole Sentence.* New Brunswick, NJ: Rutgers University Press, 2015.

Paluch, James A., Jr. *A Life for a Life.* Los Angeles: Roxbury, 2004.

CHAPTER 10   MOHAMED ATTA AND SUICIDE TERRORISTS

Benmelech, Efraim, Claude Berrebi, and Esteben Klor. "Counter-Suicide-Terrorism: Evidence from House Demolitions." *Journal of Politics* 77, no. 1 (January 2015).

Dershowitz, Alan. *Why Terrorism Works: Understanding the Threat, Responding to the Challenge.* New Haven, CT: Yale University Press, 2002.

Lewis, Bernard. *The Crisis of Islam: Holy War and Unholy Terrorism.* New York: Random House, 2003.

MacEoin, Denis. "Dimensions of Jihad: Suicide Bombing as Worship." *Middle East Quarterly* 16 no. 4 (Fall 2009).

McDermott, Terry. *Perfect Soldiers: The Hijackers—Who They Were, Why They Did It.* New York: HarperCollins, 2005.

Pape, Robert A. *Dying to Win: The Strategic Logic of Suicide Terrorism.* New York: Random House Trade Paperbacks, 2005.

CHAPTER 11   FREEDOM TO SUCCEED

Burke, Brian. "Hail Mary Probabilities." Advanced Football Analytics, September 25, 2012. http://archive.advancedfootballanalytics.com/2012/09/hail-mary-probabilities.html.

Gordon, Harry. "How the Daughter of an Ancient Race Made It Out of the Australian Outback by Hitting a Tennis Ball Sweetly and Hard." *The New York Times Magazine* (August 29, 1971): 10.

INDEX

Bush, George W., 39
Butler, Bertha, 71

C225 (cetuximab), 91
Cain, Burl, 145, 148
Cairo University, 157
California prison strike, 136–37
call option, 3, 11–12
Canary Islands, 56
cancer and experimental
    treatments, 87–89, 90–91
Capitol riot of 2021, 14
Capone, Al, 108–9
Carlson, Norman, 143
Carr, Johnnie, 69, 76
Carter, Jimmy, 44
Cartwright, James, 43–44
Cayne, James, 113
Chamberlain, Neville, 79
Chappelle, Robert M., 142
Chicago Bears, 168
Chicago Daily Tribune, 31
Chicago Mercantile Exchange, 109
China, 49, 55, 96
Christian Science Monitor, 42
Churchill, Winston, 34, 122
Cisneros, Henry, 39
Civil Rights Act, 83
Clinton, Bill, 19–20
    election of 1996, 173–74
    presidential pardons, 38–41, 46
Clinton, Hillary, 14, 39, 40
Clinton, Roger, 39
Clinton-Lewinsky scandal, 19–20
Clutts, Merle, 142–43
Coffee, John, 107
Coleman, Joe, 145
collective punishment, 162–64
Collins, Andy, 138
Columbia University, 107, 161

Columbine High School massacre,
    154
Colvin, Claudette, 65–67, 70, 71,
    73, 74
Communist Manifesto, The (Marx
    and Engels), 13
Conant, Alex, 14
Congressional Gold Medal, 63
Conner, Richard, 139–40
Convention and Protocol Relating
    to the Status of Refugees,
    50–51, 54–55, 61
Cook County Jail, 139
Coolidge, Calvin, 22
Council of Economic Advisers
    (CEA), 94–95
countervailing power, 4
Court, Margaret, 168
Coutts & Co., 100–101
COVID-19 pandemic, 92–96
    early warnings about, 3, 93–95,
    204n
    hydroxychloroquine treatment,
    85–86
Cox, Archibald, 44
Crawford, Andre, 140
Criminal Justice and Behavior, 146
Cronkite, Walter, 88
Cuba and MS *St. Louis,* 52–53
Cushing, USS, 29
Cutter, Ana, 161

Dachau concentration camp, 51,
    52–53
Dachau trials, 129
Daczewitz, Joshua, 140–41
Dalai Lama, 12
Dallas Cowboys, 172
Daugherty, Harry, 22
D.C. Blacks, 142

ABOUT THE AUTHOR

William L. Silber, the former Marcus Nadler Professor of Economics and Finance at New York University's Stern School of Business, a three-time winner of the Professor of the Year Award at Stern, is currently a senior adviser at Cornerstone Research. He received his Ph.D. in economics from Princeton University, a B.A. from Yeshiva University, and has written about financial history and monetary economics, including eight books. His most recent, *The Story of Silver: How the White Metal Shaped America and the Modern World,* called "deeply researched and authoritative" by *Kirkus Reviews,* was named a 2019 Best Book of the Year by the *Financial Times.* A previous book, *Volcker: The Triumph of Persistence,* which chronicles the career of former Federal Reserve chairman Paul Volcker, won the China Business News Financial Book of the Year in 2013, was a finalist in the Goldman Sachs/*Financial Times* Business Book of the Year in 2012, and was named "One of the Best Business Books of 2012" by Bloomberg Businessweek. His first book, *Money,* coauthored with Lawrence Ritter, made a serious topic fun to read.